Marie Van Zandt

Marie Van Zandt

THE TURBULENT CAREER OF
A BRILLIANT AMERICAN DIVA
IN EUROPE, 1879-1898

S. Lawrence Dingman & Jane Van Zandt Dingman

Copyright © 2017 S. Lawrence Dingman & Jane Van Zandt Dingman
All rights reserved.

ISBN-13: 9781539010371
ISBN-10: 1539010376
Library of Congress Control Number: 2016916034
CreateSpace Independent Publishing Platform
North Charleston, South Carolina

Contents

Preface vii

Chapter 1	Family Background and Early History, 1861–79	1
Chapter 2	Brilliant Debuts in Turin and London, 1879	7
Chapter 3	Debut at the Opéra-Comique, 1880–82	13
Chapter 4	The Creation and Premiere of *Lakmé*, 1882–83	19
Chapter 5	A Rising Star—and a "Spoiled Child," 1883	25
Chapter 6	Stardom—and Stumbles, 1884	29
Chapter 7	A Turbulent Year: Russia, Paris, and England, 1884–85	41
Chapter 8	Return to Russia, Illness, and Recuperation, 1886	62
Chapter 9	Marie and Grand Duke Michael, 1885–99	68
Chapter 10	Career and Acclaim Continue, 1887–91	74
Chapter 11	American Tour, 1891–92	91
Chapter 12	European Career Resumes, 1892–96	97
Chapter 13	A Triumphant Return to Paris, 1896	100
Chapter 14	Honors, Marriage, and Retirement, 1897–1919	109

Appendix A: Lakmé: Background, Synopsis, and Cast of the Premiere 117
Appendix B: List of Performances of American Tour 121
Appendix C: Notes, Letters, and Signed Photographs to Marie from Famous People 123
Notes 125

Preface

THIS BIOGRAPHY IS BASED LARGELY on an extensive collection of newspaper clippings, letters, event programs, and artifacts originally collected by Marie Van Zandt herself. In 1908, following the death of Marie's father in Connecticut, her brother Antonio ("Tony") crossed the Atlantic to visit Marie and their mother in France, accompanied by two of his children, Marion and Arthur. On this voyage, Arthur met Ruth Baker, his future wife, and her family. Ruth's and Marion's interest in Marie was the inspiration for this biography.

In 1920, within a year of Marie's death, Tony and Arthur traveled to Cannes and Paris to settle her estate and bring her effects to the United States. In the 1970s, Marion began to organize and translate the material and combine it with her knowledge of family history and additional research, with the intent of writing a biography of "Wissie," as Marie was known to the family. Marion never completed the task, and on her death in 1979, most of the collected materials came into the possession of Arthur and Ruth's daughter, Jane Van Zandt Dingman. Jane and her husband have compiled this biography from Marie's original materials, relying heavily on Marion's extensive notes, supplemented by historical and biographical information obtained from books and the Internet, including Wikipedia and the searchable archives of newspapers. Most of the translations from the French are by Lawrence Dingman.

We have tried to tell Wissie's story as factually as possible through the original materials, and have provided specific citations for most sources. Where details of her activities are given without citation, they are from Marion Van

Zandt's notes or from brief items reported in the Paris newspaper *Le Figaro*. There remain large gaps in the information we've obtained, some of which might be filled by more intensive searches through newspaper archives in the United States and especially Europe.

Note: After compiling our research, we became aware through the Internet of the book *Marie Van Zandt, ou le Caprice Parisienne*, identified as a "*biographie romancée*" (novelized biography) of Marie by Eric Van Zandt, which was self-published in French in 2010. M. Van Zandt is apparently related to Marie, though it is not clear how. While his book is entertaining reading and generally follows the actual events of Marie's life, it is a largely fictionalized reconstruction based on a very limited number of sources. Thus, we did not use it as a source and have not referred to it in our factual relation of Marie's life.

CHAPTER 1

Family Background and Early History, 1861–79

MARIE VAN ZANDT WAS BORN in Brooklyn, New York, in 1861. Her mother was a well-known singer whose travels to Europe led to a connection with Adelina Patti, the best-known opera singer of the day, who promoted Marie's talent. At the age of eighteen, Marie had great successes in her debuts in Italy and England. She quickly became the darling of Paris, where her capricious nature earned her the nickname *enfant gatée,* or "spoiled child." She was a brilliant singer and a charming ingénue who inspired Leo Delibes to compose the exotic opera *Lakmé* for her, and she was immensely popular with the highest levels of Parisian society. However, Marie was resented by some of the French public and perhaps by jealous colleagues, and in 1885 she became the focus of a series of near-riots in the city. Stung by this, she left Paris immediately and did not sing there again for over a decade. But she had great successes in the rest of Europe and especially in Russia, as well as in an American tour in 1891–92. From the Opéra-Comique in France to Holland, where she was given the title of "Singer of the Court;" to England, where she was a favorite of the Prince of Wales; and to Russia, where she stole the heart of the tsar's cousin; Marie Van Zandt led a life of successful artistic intrigue. She remained immensely popular until the end of her career in 1898, when she married a Russian count and settled in France.

ORIGIN MYTHS: "THE WILD CHILD"

As will be seen, Marie had amazing natural talent and became most famous for singing the roles of Mignon and Lakmé, "exotic young maidens with childish grace, charming and wild."[1] She was also known as a "spoiled child," who frequently caused difficulties for her directors and colleagues. From time to time over the course of her life, the French seem to have wanted to romanticize the origin of these qualities by attributing them to a childhood in the American wilderness, sometimes in Texas and sometimes in Massachusetts, hunting with her father and cavorting with Indians.

An example of the Texas myth appeared in a September 1883 article in *Parisiens et Parisiennes*:

> Marie Van Zandt was born in the Far West…Her father had a large property in the forests of Texas. His daughter was raised among tattooed Indians [and] wild bison…At the age of four she went with her father on hunts, riding behind him on his horse; later, mounted on a great horse, she visited Indian encampments alone…[2]

There is a Van Zandt County in Texas about thirty miles east of Dallas, that was formed in 1848 and named for Isaac Van Zandt, who was a member of the congress of the Republic of Texas.[3] This is likely the reason for the supposed connection with Marie; however, there is no known actual or plausible connection between that county and Marie's family. Beth Gordon of the Genealogical Society of Van Zandt County, Texas, told us, "We have no record of a Marie Van Zandt ever living in Van Zandt County."

The Massachusetts version of Marie's wild-child myth appeared in *Le Figaro*'s review of the premiere of *Lakmé* on April 15, 1883,[4] and was repeated in its brief obituary of her on January 14, 1920:

> Her parents rented a country house in Groton, Massachusetts, and there, from morning until evening, the mignon Marie wandered the forests, competing with the birds in singing, awakening echoes with her triumphant melodies. A large troupe of Indians came to camp in these woods, whose chief was called Venicalita. The Indians followed her, charmed by her voice, and considered the young singer with her pale face a supernatural being. When she was only six years old, she had cast such a spell on these Indians that they would have given their lives for her twenty times over…[5]

Groton is only thirty-five miles from Boston and by 1863 had been settled by people of European descent for over two centuries; it was incorporated in 1655.[6] Thus, there were no large troupes of Indians living there in the 1860s, and the details of this version of her origin seem entirely fanciful.

But Marie actually did have a connection to Groton, Massachusetts. As the following excerpt indicates, she lived there as a child at the house of her maternal grandfather, Antonio Blitz, and his second wife for some period:

> The house on Main St. next north of Moison's Hardware store was the home of Jonas and Eliza (Adams) Eaton in 1863, when their daughter Helen Eliza was married to Signor Antonio Blitz. The ceremony was performed at the house on July 23, 1863. Helen was the second wife of Signor Blitz, who was a well known ventriloquist or "thaumaturgist." A granddaughter of his was Mademoiselle Marie Van Zandt, a noted prima donna in her day, "and during her childhood she passed many months at Mr. Eaton's dwelling, and attended school in town."[7]

THE TRUE STORY

Marie Louise Van Zandt was descended from one of the early Knickerbocker families of New York. The first to emigrate from Holland was Wynant Van Zandt in 1649. One of his descendants, also named Wynant Van Zandt (1761–1831), settled in Little Neck (Long Island), New York, and married Mary Underhill in 1788. One of their eleven sons was Robert Benson Van Zandt (1799–1844), who was brought up in Little Neck. Robert married Mary Hicks (1801–82), and the ninth of their ten children was James Rose Van Zandt (ca. 1835–1907). On June 11, 1855, James Rose married Jane Blitz (1836–1913) of Philadelphia, the daughter of Antonio Blitz ("Signor Blitz"), a well-known magician and ventriloquist, and his first wife (née Morrison). Their children, all born at 49 Willoughby Avenue in Brooklyn, were Amelia (Millie, 1856–193?), Antonio (Tony, later called Dudley, 1858–1941), and Marie Louise (Wissie), who was born on October 16, 1861.[8]

Jane Blitz was said to have a lovely mezzo-soprano voice and was a soloist in church and in the Handel and Haydn Society of Boston. She sang in several operas, soirées, and benefit concerts in New York from 1863 to 1865. She was advised to go to Europe to study for opera, and sometime, probably in 1865, the family crossed the Atlantic on a Cunard side-wheeler. Jane studied with Francesco Lamperti in Milan, one of the best-known teachers of the time. Following this, Jane Blitz Van Zandt, under the name of Jennie Vanzini, sang with the Carl Rosa Opera Company in Copenhagen (1865), Warsaw (1866), Milan (La Scala, 1867–68), and London (Covent Garden, 1868–70). As noted above, Marie apparently lived at the home of her maternal grandfather in Massachusetts for some period after 1863. But for some of her early childhood, Marie and her siblings were educated in France and England while their mother pursued her career. During this time, Jennie became a close friend of two of the most famous opera singers of the day, Adelina Patti and Christine Nilsson.

Figure 1. Program for the Clara Louise Kellogg production of *Martha*, starring Jennie Van Zandt, May 6, 1874, at the American Academy of Music, Philadelphia.

Jennie and Tony returned to the United States, arriving in New York on September 23, 1873,[9] and during 1873–75, Jennie toured with Clara Louise Kellogg's English Opera Troupe, singing operas in English in Boston and other cities (fig. 1). These translated operas were extremely popular at the time; some of those in her repertoire were *Faust, Martha, Carmen, The Bohemian Girl*, and *Rigoletto*. It was in this same year that Marie, aged eleven and a half, first sang a solo in public:

> It was at a May festival in Rutland, Vt., in May 1873.[10] She led a chorus of three hundred little girls, singing the solo parts in a childish voice of singular sweetness and power.[11]

Sometime around 1875, Jennie and the children returned to Europe, probably to London, where Jennie continued her career (fig. 2). During this period, Marie's native singing ability became increasingly apparent, and Adelina Patti brought her to the attention of J. H. Mapleson, director of Her Majesty's Theatre, London, when she was but thirteen years of age:

Figure 2. Jennie Vanzini of the Carl Rosa Opera Company on the cover of *The Illustrated Sporting & Dramatic News* of London, March 8, 1879.

Mme. Adelina Patti...pronounced [Marie's] abilities to be phenomenal and predicted that she would be a prominent artist and "my successor" as the diva expressed it. At this early age she sang in the Drury Lane Theatre the Jewel Song from *Faust*, "Voi che sapete"...to the wonder and delight of her hearers, the most enthusiastic of whom was Adelina Patti. She was, however, advised by physicians to abstain from singing and was sent to school in Brighton, England.[12]

Such extravagant praise from one of the most famous sopranos in history[13] prompted Jennie to turn from her own career to concentrate on cultivating Marie's talent. The two older children, Amelia and Antonio, were sent to boarding school in England.

James Rose and Jane separated at some point, probably when Jane started her European singing career or soon after. James returned to the United States and later lived with his son Tony and family in New York and New Canaan, Connecticut. Tony had returned to the United States after his schooling in Leamington, England, while Jennie and the girls made their home in France, probably in Nice and/or Paris. Jennie soon gave up her singing career entirely and devoted herself to Marie. At one point, however, it is reported that they sang together in the opera *Martha* in London.

In late 1878 and early 1879, Marie studied for six months at the Milan Conservatory with her mother's former teacher, the famous Lamperti. However, it appears that she was very largely taught by her mother during their travels, and she knew many roles before her formal training began. From an early age, Marie had a remarkable ability to learn opera parts quickly and sing them perfectly. Thus, although it was noted in several later news reports that Marie shunned rehearsals and often begged sickness to avoid them, she was always fully prepared to sing in performance—except, as we shall see, in one troubling incident in Paris in 1884.

CHAPTER 2

Brilliant Debuts in Turin and London, 1879

ON MARCH 15, 1879, AT the age of seventeen and a half, Marie Van Zandt made her first professional opera appearance as Zerlina in Mozart's *Don Giovanni* at the Teatro Regio in Turin, Italy. She was very well received, as reflected in this review:

> Here we have a Zerlina (Miss Van Zandt), who is a pretty bauble, tiny, a *bijou*, with a pleasant voice and a certain grace that one falls in love with.[14]

News of this success quickly spread, and Col. Mapleson engaged Marie to appear in that same role at Her Majesty's Theatre, London. News of her English debut was announced in early May:

> Another interesting debut will be that of Marie Van Zandt (Mlle. Vanzini), a very youthful soprano of whom the highest expectations are formed, and who last month made a brilliantly successful first appearance in Turin as Zerlina in *Il Don Giovanni*.[15]

The first English review appeared the day after the performance:

> She is young and pretty, and although she has little stage experience there is a certain charm about her acting. Her voice is a pure soprano, more remarkable for sweetness than power. Her intonation is

excellent, her phrasing good. The success she achieved is legitimate and genuine.[16]

On May 7, the *London Daily News* echoed these comments and added that

> She has an excellent *sostenuto*, the latter being especially welcome in these days of almost universal *tremolo*. Her stage manner was extremely good, notwithstanding some nervousness. Having presented the rustic coquette with artless simplicity and vivacity without flippancy, the arias "Bati-Bati" and "Bedrai Carino" were charmingly rendered, both having been encored, as was the duet with Don Giovanni, "La ci darem."[17]

On May 8, illness prevented Etelka Gerster from appearing in her usual role as Amina in Bellini's *La Sonnambula*, and Christina Nilsson was also indisposed and unavailable to substitute for her. Marie was proposed as a last-minute substitute and accepted the challenge, even though she had never played the part before. This must have been an exceptionally stressful debut for the young Marie, because ailments also affected the scheduled male lead and three potential substitutes. The *Manchester Guardian* of May 9 gave an amusing account—one that itself seems suitable as a basis for an opera!

> Mlle. Gerster was to have come out tonight as Amina…, but the famous Hungarian *prima donna* is suffering from bronchitis. Mme. Nilsson is confined to her house with…rheumatism…Mlle. Van Zandt, the youthful daughter of…Mme. Vanzini, who made so successful a debut as Zerlina in *Don Giovanni* last Saturday, was ready to undertake the character of Amina. But Sir Michael Costa thought it hazardous to entrust a novice—a mere child—with so arduous a part. After hearing her, however, in the two principal airs he changed his mind, and Signor Campanini was summoned to rehearse with Mlle. Van Zandt the part of Elbino. Campanini had something the matter with his throat, and pleaded *"maladie de larynx."* Then Signor Frapoli

was sent for. But Frapoli's bronchial tubes were somehow affected, and he also could not sing. He began a rehearsal, but after a time was obliged to give up. Signor Runcio was now applied to, but Mlle. Van Zandt had not gone through much of the opera with this new Elbino when he declared himself unable to continue. The game was not yet lost, for Mr. Mapleson had still one tenor in reserve, an eminent vocalist named Brignoll, who when he was in his prime, could sing the part of Elbino perfectly, and who can sing effectively enough even now. Brignoll, however, was found to be afflicted with an absolute extinction of voice. He could neither sing nor even attempt to sing. Mr. Mapleson's company is strong in tenors, but a director cannot be expected to have more than four tenors in his troupe to whom such a part as that of Elbino could be confided, and four possible Elbinos had all fallen victims to the persistent bad weather. It was out of the question to borrow a tenor from Mr. Gye; the manager of the Royal Italian Opera would naturally not lend one. At last, someone in the theatre mentioned that Signor Carrion—a tenor who sang at Her Majesty's Theatre quite lately, but who no longer belongs to the company—but who was in London, and a messenger was at once dispatched to Signor Carrion's hotel with orders to seize him and bring him, willing or unwilling, to rehearsal. Signor Carrion, oddly enough, was *not* ill—his throat, bronchial tubes, and all, was in perfect condition—but he was in bed, and refused to get up. Probably he thought by declining to move he would force the distressed manager to offer him an engagement for a term of years. He would not, in any case, leave his bed. At last, however, he was compelled to get up and was brought to the theatre. Some sort of costume was found for him and the rehearsal proceeded. The performance has now taken place. Mlle. Van Zandt has sung with brilliant success—such a success as no Amina has obtained since the debut of Adelina Patti in this charming part; but nothing seemed more probable this morning—when four different tenors were found to have been incapacitated by our weather—than that it would not take place at all. Mlle. Van Zandt revealed a sweetness and brilliancy of execution which will assuredly win for her the highest honours of the lyric stage. So petite an embodiment of the girlish heroine of Bellini's opera and vocalisations so graceful and exquisitely tender have rarely been combined; and when the age of the artist is considered, the performance is truly marvelous and shows the inspiration of true genius.[18]

The significance of Marie's excellent performance on stepping into the role of Amina at very short notice was highlighted in this May 12 article:

Owing to illness that precluded the possibility of Mme. Gerster appearing in *La Sonnambula*, for which she had been announced on Thursday, such a chance as may not happen to an *ingénue* in a century, was given to Mlle. Van Zandt, who, at a day's notice, was called upon to personate and sing the elaborate music of the heroine in that opera…The little lady had never appeared in the part of Amina on any stage previously but, in spite of such a disadvantage, she both acted and sang as if she were an *artiste* of double her years. Her phrasing was perfect, her singing…invariably neat and delicately true, her manner natural and modest, and her entire realization of the demands of her part and of the scene something marvelous when her youth is taken into account and it is remembered that until six weeks ago, when she appeared at Turin, no public could have believed that such a prodigy was about to burst upon them.…We [were at] the debut of Mme. Patti in the same opera, and what we said after that most successful debut to the late Mr. Gye, we will now repeat to Mr. Mapleson: "You have obtained the most promising musical genius that has for many a long day come before the public…We have no hesitation in saying that the promise of Mme. Patti's first appearance was by no means so promising as that which Mlle. Van Zandt has given."[19]

On June 7, Marie appeared as Cherubino in *The Marriage of Figaro*. Marie's "Newspaper Cuttings" scrapbook contains over seventy-five clippings from May and June 1879 that, without exception, give her performances in all these roles extremely high praise. During this period, she also gave a subscription-night performance of *Il Don Giovanni* on May 22 (fig. 3) and on June 25, she was part of a "Grand Morning Concert" in aid of London's Great Northern Hospital, in which she sang a solo and a duet (fig. 4).

Figure 3. Newspaper announcement of subscription-night performance of *Il Don Giovanni* on May 22, 1879.

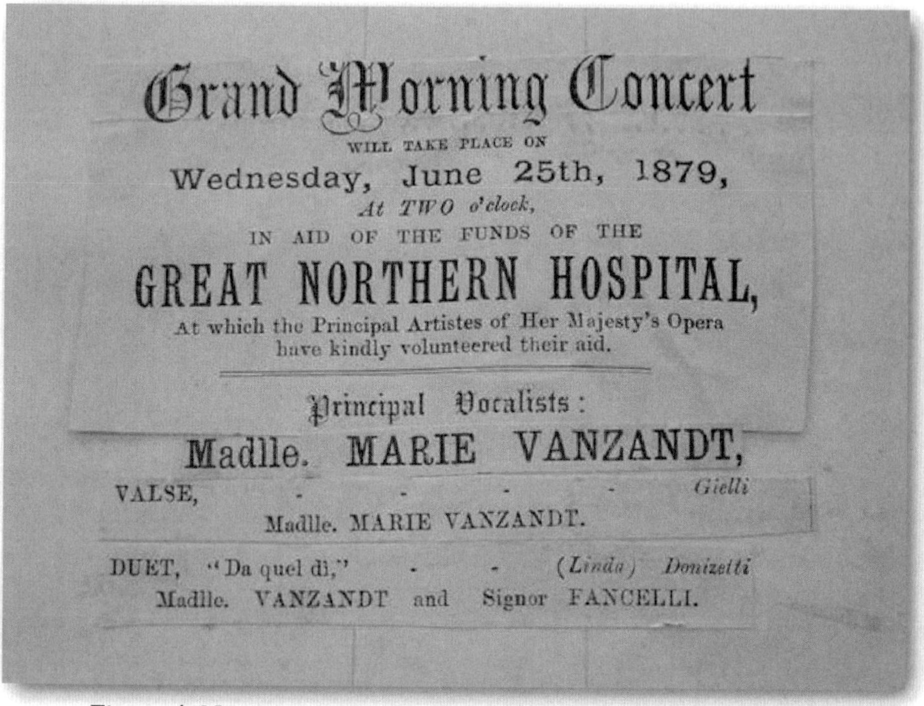

Grand Morning Concert
WILL TAKE PLACE ON
Wednesday, June 25th, 1879,
At TWO o'clock,
IN AID OF THE FUNDS OF THE
GREAT NORTHERN HOSPITAL,
At which the Principal Artistes of Her Majesty's Opera
have kindly volunteered their aid.

Principal Vocalists:
Madlle. MARIE VANZANDT,

VALSE, - - - - *Gielli*
Madlle. MARIE VANZANDT.

DUET, "Da quel di," - - *(Linda) Donizetti*
Madlle. VANZANDT and Signor FANCELLI.

Figure 4. Newspaper announcement of "Grand Morning Concert" in aid of London's Great Northern Hospital, June 25, 1879.

CHAPTER 3

Debut at the Opéra-Comique, 1880–82

FOLLOWING THESE SUCCESSES, MAPLESON OFFERED Marie a tour of America, and by November 1879 she had also received an offer to sing in Saint Petersburg. However, in December she chose to accept the offer of the director, Léon Carvalho, of the Paris Opéra-Comique (fig. 5), made on the recommendations of Adelina Patti and Christine Nilsson. She auditioned before Carvalho, his opera-singer wife Mme. Miolan-Carvalho, *Mignon* composer Ambroise Thomas and others. It was decided that she would make her Opéra-Comique debut as Mignon, following which she would appear as Dinorah in Meyerbeer's *The Pardon of Ploermal*, Amina in *La Sonnambula*, and Cherubino in *The Marriage of Figaro*.

Figure 5. Façade of the Opéra-Comique (Second "Salle Favart,"[20] 1840–87)

On February 25, 1880, less than three weeks before her debut, Marie appeared at a ball at the Elysée Palace in Paris that was described in the *Philadelphia Evening Telegraph*[21] as "one of the most brilliant that had ever been given at the Elysée," with many prominent Americans present. The *Telegraph* described her gown in great detail: "white crepe and satin with clusters of pale pink roses and lace" and noted that "the beauty of our fair young prima donna attracted much attention." Figure 6 is a photograph of Marie at about this time.

Figure 6. Portrait of Marie by Van Bosch, Paris, 1880 or 1881.

On March 18, Marie made her Opéra-Comique debut (under the name of Marie Vanza) as Mignon, with Patti, Nilsson, and many American officials and wealthy expatriates in attendance. Her performance was judged a great success, as reported in over thirty newspaper clippings in her scrapbook. The one from the *Continental Gazette* of March 20 gives the flavor of these reviews:

> The debut of the American prima-donna, Marie Van Zandt at the Opéra-Comique...resulted in a complete and brilliant success. She appeared as Mignon in Ambroise Thomas's well known opera. Her rendition of the air "Knowst thou the land" called forth long applause. But the "Styrienne" in the second act fairly carried the audience captive and awakened that low-toned murmur or rather thrill of applause which in a French audience is far more significant of delight than many bravos. Young as Mlle. Van Zandt is, she is only just 19 [actually, she was 18], she is already an artiste. She manages her singularly pure and sympathetic voice with wonderful skill, disdaining with rare judgment to sacrifice the true character of the music to tinsel or overstrained ornamentation. She is also possessed of remarkable dramatic power and her child-like beauty and grace added greatly to the charm of her rendition. The house was crowded in every part. The American colony was...represented...in its entirety. The U.S. minister, General Noyes...our First Secretary of Legation...acting Consul-General...and many other Americans were present. General and Mrs. Noyes sent their warmest congratulations to the young performer...There was also a brilliant array of operatic celebrities among the audience: Mme. Patti, Mme. Nilsson, Mme. Miolan-Carvalho, and Miss Kellogg among the most noted. M. Ambroise Thomas was also present and watched with eyes of keen and animated interest every movement and gesture of this, the latest and youngest of his Mignons. He has from the very beginning manifested the deepest interest in the talents of this gifted child and the care and attention that he bestowed on the rehearsals must have been largely repaid by the result. The house presented a most attractive spectacle, all the ladies on the first tier and in the boxes being in full dress. With the remarkable good taste and judgment that characterizes all Mlle. Van

Zandt's proceedings, she had requested her friends to abstain from any floral offerings to her while she was on the stage. Her wish was respected, but her dressing room was crowded with superb and fragrant bouquets, the genuine homage of true friendship and heartfelt enthusiasm.[22]

We have no information about Marie's activities until March 1881, when she returned to the Opéra-Comique stage in *Mignon*. On April 13 (Easter Sunday), her "ravishing voice"[23] was heard at a soirée at the home of M. Campbell-Clarke, the Paris correspondent for the London *Daily Telegraph*. In May she appeared in *Figaro* and in *The Pardon of Ploermal*, for which she also received high praise:

> Mlle. Marie Van Zandt played, for the first time, the long and difficult part of Dinorah…This evening has been a real triumph for Mlle. Van Zandt, who lends to that touching figure of the goat-keeper the charm of her precious qualities, both as a woman and an artist. Meyerbeer has certainly not dreamt of a Dinorah more talented and more poetic. It is a revelation, the vision of this quite young artist who in a few months knew how to conquer so many sympathies and find an entire public to applaud her. Already one compares her to Patti, but especially to Nilsson…It is impossible to sing a musical phrase with more feeling and clarity; impossible to vocalize with more boldness. Her voice is clear, limpid, and easy…A new star has risen in the artistic heavens of the Opéra-Comique. May she shine a long time.[24]

She continued singing Mignon and Dinorah at the Opéra-Comique for the rest of that season, but there were newspaper reports that she was "indisposed" and could not sing on several occasions, causing some friction between her and Carvalho. However, she remained very popular, and the May 14 edition of the Paris weekly *Camées Artistiques* was devoted to Marie (fig. 7); its review of her Mignon said

[Her] success was unquestionable. One found oneself face to face with a girl of 18 years, with a slender adolescent figure, with a lively face, with brusque staccato gestures, a true Mignon, sweet and savage at the same time, delicate and straightforward, such that one loves to dream as one follows her across her thoughts of her immortal creator. Her voice is sustained, with an agreeable timbre, that handles difficulties without effort; all combining to make this young stranger very agreeable; the name of Nilsson could be mentioned as a term of comparison.[25]

Figure 7. Marie as Mignon. From *Camées Artistiques* No. 54, May 14, 1881.

As we will see, Marie became perhaps even more identified with the role of Mignon than with that of Lakmé, which was written especially for her a few years later.

Occasional newspaper reports indicate that Marie was in Paris for most of 1881 and was back at the Opéra-Comique singing in *Mignon* and *The Pardon of Ploermel* in the fall of that year. However, an 1882 clipping says Marie had great success in *Figaro* in Denmark "last season"—presumably 1881—and among her surviving possessions is an inscribed gold bracelet from Queen Louise of Denmark (fig. 8).

Figure 8. Left: Bracelet inscribed with the opening words of Mignon's Act I aria "*Connais-tu le pays où fleurit l'oranger? Le pays des fruits d'or et des roses vermeilles.*" Courtesy of Susan R. [Van Zandt] Ferraro. Right: Bracelet engraved "fra (from) Dronning (Queen) Louise of Denmark to Marie Van Zandt." Center: Marie's wedding ring.

In late January and early February 1882, Marie gave two special concert performances before leaving for a two-week engagement in the south of France. She sang in Monte-Carlo and Nice, after which she returned to the Opéra-Comique to appear in *Figaro* and *Mignon* in late February—and apparently for the rest of that season and the next. In October it was announced that Marie was beginning to rehearse *Lakmé*, which Léo Delibes had been writing for her.

CHAPTER 4

The Creation and Premiere of *Lakmé*, 1882–83

MANY REVIEWS OF MARIE'S SINGING at the Opéra-Comique noted her clear high notes, her youth, her exotic aspect, and her fresh, unaffected acting. Because of these qualities and her extraordinary success, especially as Mignon, it was reported that no fewer than six composers were writing operas especially for her.[26] However, the only one actually completed was *Lakmé*.

Inspired by Marie's singing, Edmond Gondinet and Philippe Gille developed a French libretto based on an 1880 autobiographical novel by Pierre Loti, *Le Mariage de Loti*. For the music they approached Léo Delibes (1836–91), with whom they had worked before and who had composed the well-known ballets *Coppélia* (1870) and *Sylvie* (1876) and the operas *Le Roi l'A Dit* (1873) and *Jean de Nivelle* (1880).

Set in British India in the mid-nineteenth century,

> *Lakmé* utilizes the most efficient forces of orientalist opera: as with David and Massenet, it is a musical reverie on a remote civilization; as with Bizet, the confrontation between religious fanaticism and exacerbated sensuality; as with Meyerbeer, it includes the passion of two lovers from different cultures. In a lush background that combines wild nature and popular festivities, the encounter of a Brahman's daughter and a British officer rekindles the tensions between communities in British India. Inspired by Pierre Loti, Léo Delibes transcends conventions through the truthfulness of his characters, the poetry of each scene and the importance of political questioning.[27]

A more extensive synopsis and background of the opera is given in appendix A.

Delibes worked on the score for eleven months, and completed it in June 1882. However, because Marie had other commitments, the premiere was delayed until the following spring. Rehearsals began in October 1882, and apparently Marie proved to be a temperamental star, causing the composer and director considerable anxiety while preparing for the premiere:

> At first, Mlle. Van Zandt, by contract, wants to play only twice a week. She goes to parties, to balls, in the clubs and sings when she pleases. But for the theatre it is another thing. She pretends that her health does not allow her to sing more than eight times a month. And one must be happy when she is willing to give these eight times. How often it happens that at six o'clock in the evening, without notice, without explanation, she announces that she is not going to sing that evening. They send doctors! The doctors declare that the warbler, Van Zandt, is miraculously well. But the warbler Van Zandt has decided, and one must not think of making her go back on her decision! Perhaps if she could be paid more, would she consent to have better health? But until she notices that without the Opéra-Comique she would not exist and that in leaving the Opéra-Comique she would lose a great part of her prestige; one must, however, accept her capriciousness without saying anything.
>
> Furthermore, if Mlle. Van Zandt sings only twice a week, she hardly rehearses twice a month. Delibes accepted willingly that his play would be given only twice a week, but he wanted at least that it would be rehearsed. But, ah no…There were certain duets that Mlle. Van Zandt sang only the evening of the final rehearsal. Previously, when she sang her duet with Mme. Carvalho in *The Marriage of Figaro*, she sang without any rehearsal at all. If Delibes was worrying, you can understand it, because he is punctual, methodical, timid, and does not want to leave anything to chance.
>
> Last week, when everything was about ready, Mlle. Van Zandt made it known that she needed three weeks of rest before creating her role and that she was going to take a trip. This time M. Carvalho got angry. The very next day, he made Mlle. Van Zandt sing Mignon, which she should not have played again until next year, and declared…that if

she refused, he would leave it to the public to be a judge and would post a notice: "Postponed on account of the refusal of Mlle. Van Zandt to play." At the same time, he made the orchestra rehearse *Carmen* to have this work ready to replace the new work, which would be postponed until next year with Mlle. Nevada playing Lakmé. Mlle. Van Zandt became frightened. She yielded, and from that time on has been as mild as a lamb. How long will this obedience last? No one can say.[28]

Lakmé premiered on April 14, 1883, at the Opéra-Comique under the direction of Léon Carvalho, with Jules Danbé conducting and the well-known tenor Jean-Alexandre Talazac playing opposite Marie as Gérald (figs. 9 and 10). There was great acclaim for the work and for Marie:

> The young singer is absolutely ravishing in this strange character. The readers of *Parliment* know that I am not a blind admirer of the young American diva. If I have applauded her debut in *Mignon*, I did not miss criticizing her in *The Pardon of Ploermal* and *The Marriage of Figaro*, but this time I must admit that she has completely subjugated me. She has composed her part with an intelligence that shines in the smallest details and she not only sings it delightfully, but she plays it with great art. There is indeed in this child a superior dramatic instinct which makes her find the right gesture and movement and gives to her public a command which cannot be denied.[29]

> Mlle. Van Zandt is not satisfied to shed all the pearls of her dazzling soprano, she plays [her part] as a real actress, gifted with a rare intelligence and artistic temperament, original and impulsive…[30]

> Mlle. Van Zandt displayed an exceptional voice which reached the highest "E" with ease and tenderness, a voice which has no rival since Patti and Nilsson…It is especially important to note the intelligence, the grace, and the sensitivity that she has shown in creating the adorable character of Lakmé, which is embodied in her…Van Zandt is exactly the exotic character, with childish grace, charming and wild, of

which the authors of *Lakmé* were dreaming…Van Zandt is the most charming singer, the spoiled child of the public, whose Lakmé puts her among the most exquisite artists of the day.³¹

[W]hen one sees her, when one hears her, this little unruly one, this spoiled and terrible child, one must admit that one must forgive all her follies and her unreasonableness. She is bewitching to the last degree, with her great inexperience, her blinding faults; but also with her marvelous instinct of the stage, her admirable understanding of the theatre, and her easy and adorable voice. There were certain attitudes, certain movements, certain flashes that Mlle. Van Zandt had last night which reveal, positively, a great artist. Perhaps, if she were less capricious she would be less adorable. Let us, then draw a veil over these failures and be content to acclaim her as she deserves.³²

Figure 9. Marie as Lakmé, 1883: (a) Benque & Co., Paris; (b) from Gallica. bnf.fr/Bibliothèque national de France; (c) and (d), Van Bosch, Paris.

Figure 10. Program, ticket stub, and photograph from Paris Opéra-Comique, October 12, 1883. From *Opera News* (Metropolitan Opera Guild), vol. 11, no. 5, November 18, 1946.

Since its premiere, *Lakmé* has been performed fifteen hundred times at the Opéra-Comique, most recently on January 10–20, 2014. It was scheduled to make its American premiere at the New York Metropolitan Opera during the 1884–85 season, with both Emma Nevada and Etelka Gerster vying for the title role, but it was canceled because of a copyright disagreement. The actual American premiere was on March 1, 1886, by the American Opera Company in New York. In April 1890, the New York Metropolitan Opera staged an Italian version of the opera, with the famous Adelina Patti starring. However, her performance and the production were severely panned. *Lakmé* in the original French did not enter the Metropolitan's repertoire until February 22, 1892, with Marie Van Zandt herself starring. Her voice and acting apparently still had their original qualities, as the *New York Times* review praised "her light and pretty voice and facile execution.[33]" Since then, the Met has presented *Lakmé* sixty-two times, most recently when it opened the 1946–47 season with Lily Pons starring (fig. 11). It is revived from time to time around the world, as by the Montreal Opera in May 2007 and the Australian Opera in 2012.

Figure 11. Program for Metropolitan Opera performance of *Lakmé*, November 23, 1946. From *Opera News* (Metropolitan Opera Guild), vol. 11, no. 5, November 18, 1946.

CHAPTER 5

A Rising Star—and a "Spoiled Child," 1883

IN LATE JANUARY 1883, WHILE the premiere of *Lakmé* was being prepared, Marie traveled to Monte Carlo, where she sang in *Faust* and, as reported in *Le Figaro*, also indulged her penchant for roulette. (The newspaper reported that her favorite numbers to play were 14, 16, 22, 25, and 29.[34]) She returned to Paris to continue to play at the Opéra-Comique in *Mignon* and in a revival of *The Marriage of Figaro* while preparing *Lakmé*. Remarkably, on April 15, the day after her *Lakmé* debut, she sang in a soirée to an audience of the highest members of French society at the "vast mansion"[35] of the ninety-four-year-old Duchess of Albuféra, who had been a friend of Napoleon's Empress Josephine. In May Marie sang one of her songs from *Lakmé* at a "Japanese Festival" in Paris. During the remainder of the 1882–83 season, Marie continued to appear in *Mignon* and *Figaro* as well as in *Lakmé*, to continued high praise.

After the season, Marie spent some days in Deauville, a resort on the English Channel, with her sister Amelia and presumably her mother. The new star's activities there and immediately afterward were reported in some detail by *Le Figaro*.[36] Her stay was intended to be a vacation, but she was talked into giving a recital at which she sang several songs, including an English tune on which she accompanied herself on the piano. She also had an avid interest in betting on the horse racing there.

As the 1883–84 season was to begin, the temperamental nature that had become evident during the rehearsals for *Lakmé* was beginning to give Marie a reputation as an *enfant gatée*—a spoiled child. This reputation was enhanced by her mysterious behavior in early September 1883 when she went to Hamburg for unknown reasons. From there she informed Carvalho on

September 6 that she was indisposed and would be unable to return by the fifteenth to make the scheduled reopening of *Lakmé*. Carvalho repeatedly telegraphed her to request that she fulfill her contractual agreement. In response she notified him, and the public, through a letter in *Le Figaro* that a German doctor had certified that "Mlle. Van Zandt is ill and unable to sing before October 1." Carvalho responded with his own public (and somewhat sarcastic) letter on the fifteenth, in which he doubted her inability to sing, requested that she return to be examined by one of the Opéra-Comique's physicians, and forcefully reminded her of her contractual obligations.[37] She was chided by *Le Figaro* for selfishly creating a "fla-fla,"[38] and she did return on September 24, making light of the fracas:

> Mlle. Van Zandt is quite reestablished, and with a charming cheerfulness…As soon as the interview was over, she bounded into her coach, appearing to be no more than 15 years old, and wearing a petite, highly original jockey's blouse, created especially for her by a fashionable couturier, and it was truly difficult not to be seduced by the charm of this ravishing American, the *enfant gatée* of the Parisian public.[39]

Lakmé reopened on September 26, to an audience consisting of "very few Parisians and enormous numbers of the highest echelon of the foreign colony,[40]" and Marie was indeed reestablished:

> Is there any need to say that people gave Van Zandt the welcome of an *enfant gatée*? The public does not hold a grudge against artists whom they love, and Van Zandt is counted among those they love most. Lakmé was feted, acclaimed; during the two intermissions there was a long procession of friends and enthusiastic admirers, and her dressing room was full of flowers. Never had she sung better, never had she been more touching, more truly dramatic. She…sang her major aria of the second act with a nobility, a surety of execution, a purity of voice and of style that won her long applause…After her triumph of this evening, I believe Van Zandt is as happy to be back as people are to see her again.[41]

Lakmé was such a success that its run was extended for a month to January 14.

During this period, Marie was being offered proposals to sing elsewhere, and was in negotiations for an American tour:

> Mlle. Van Zandt said that, during her vacation, she had refused several offers from directors who said that they would pay to free her of her current obligations and give her whatever salary she asked. But she had accepted an offer to sing next year at the new Metropolitan Opera in New York for a fee of 750,000 francs and the expenses of four people in her entourage for seven months. When asked about who would replace her at the Opéra-Comique, she said that she asked nothing more than that any of her comrades who did so would have the same success that she has had. And she added, "As for Lakmé, I do not want anyone else to play that role as long as I am at the Opéra-Comique."[42]

However, on October 13, *Le Figaro* reported that although Marie had not yet signed a contract for an American tour, "one must consider as certain the engagement of Marie Van Zandt in the United States—next year."[43] This also turned out not to be true, and in fact, Marie did not sing in America until the 1891–92 season.

On November 8, 1883, Marie was among the many stars of the theater and opera who performed at a celebration of the retirement of the actress and comedienne Anaïs Fargueil from fifty years on the French stage. Marie sang "with inexpressible charm"[44] "Les Enfants," a poem that had recently been set to music by Jules Massenet, professor at the Paris Conservatory and composer of *Manon* and many other operas, as well as other works. He had written her the day before the celebration in the note shown below, "I say again that I am very proud and very happy that you will sing 'Les Enfants.' I thank you with all my heart." He also sent his regards to her mother (fig. 12).

The great success of *Lakmé* must have erased Delibes's frustrations with the young *enfant gatée*, as he sent her a musical "Merry Christmas" note, signed and dated December 25 (fig. 13).

Figure 12. Note from Jules Massenet to Marie, November 7, 1883.

Figure 13. Christmas note from Léo Delibes to Marie, December 25, 1883.

CHAPTER 6

Stardom—and Stumbles, 1884

THE YEAR 1884 WAS A turbulent one for Marie. As we have seen, her remarkable singing and charming, unaffected acting, especially as Mignon and Lakmé, had captivated Paris. These qualities also attracted many prominent people in England, and she returned to London at the close of the 1883–84 season, apparently on vacation. She clearly had previously established close relationships with some of the most notable British musicians, including Sir Arthur Sullivan, and had become a favorite of the Prince and Princess of Wales. Unfortunately, we don't know much about these relationships, but correspondence from the summer of 1884 indicates that she had turned down invitations to dine with and sing for the Prince and Princess and was concerned about their possible displeasure. Apparently, all was resolved, as she was back in the royal good graces a year later. She returned to the Opéra-Comique for the 1884–85 season, and it was there that the most unfortunate incident of her career occurred—the result of simple stage fright, an overdose of a tonic, or a plot by jealous colleagues?

THE TOAST OF PARIS

As 1884 began, Marie Van Zandt was the toast of Paris. On January 3, a reporter for *Le Figaro* interviewed her in her apartment, which he described as being filled with hundreds of flowers and expensive gifts from admirers, including jewels, a carved cabinet, an enameled clock, and "a book of beautiful baby pictures in remembrance of the way she sang 'Les Enfants'"[45] (presumably from Massenet).

The last performance of *Lakmé* was on January 14. On February 4, after renewing her contract to perform at the Opéra-Comique, Marie left Paris for six weeks. This was not a vacation: she was praised for her performance in *The Pardon of Ploermal* in Nice on February 15; on March 3, she performed *Lakmé* in Lyon, where the *Courrier de Lyon* reported that "the voice of Mlle. Van Zandt is delightful, full, brilliant, steady, with a suppleness that has no equal...Everything is executed to perfection."[46]; and on March 16, she received seven curtain calls for her performance in *Lakmé* in Geneva. *Le Figaro* reported that Marie received 4,000 francs per performance on this tour.[47]

While she was on the tour, *Le Figaro* announced that Marie had contracted to play in *Lakmé, Mignon, The Pardon of Ploermel*, and *The Marriage of Figaro* in Russia for the 1884–85 season.[48] Clearly, her fame was spreading rapidly. In a letter dated March 10, 1884, the Master of Chapelle for the King of Holland invited Marie to sing for the court, and on March 16 she received a telegram from the Dutch court asking if she had received that letter. We have no information about if or when she sang in the land of her ancestors, but in a certificate dated March 17, 1884, Marie Van Zandt was named "Singer of the Court" by the King of Holland, a very rare honor (fig. 14).

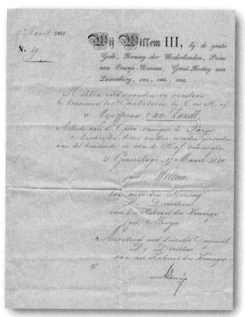

Figure 14. Certificate from King William III of the Netherlands naming "Mejuffrouw (Mademoiselle) van Zandt" a "Singer of the Court," March 17, 1884.

On March 27, 1884, Marie returned from her tour to finish the current season at the Opéra-Comique[49] and was exuberantly welcomed by this poem in *Le Gauloise* on April 1[50]:

The Return of VAN ZANDT in *MIGNON*

Do you know the diva who, to go down
To the land of golden fruit and vermillion grapes,
Fled from Paris, torn out of our arms,
Into the land of the Niçois to caress their ears;
Whose figure is so lithe it vexes the reeds;
Whose voice is so charming it troubles the birds?
    Alas! To follow that beauty
    I would give all the gold amassed by Zola.
    She is here,
    It is Van Zandt to whom I call;
    She returns, she is here.
    She is here, it is Van Zandt to whom I call,
    Here, she is here!

Do you know the sweet sound of bravos so flattering,
The sound that makes five fingers tap on a palm,
The delicious sound made by the audience
Who, because of her art, grant the artist royalty?
At the Opéra-Comique, yesterday, I heard this,
The sound which, to the audience, seemed like paradise.
Van Zandt, may heaven deliver you
From your traveling instinct which so desolates us?
    It is here
    It is here that you must be,
    To captivate and to remain, it is here!
    It is here that you must be,
    It is here! Yes, it is here!

As in earlier years, critics continued to praise her special affinity for the part of Mignon:

> [I]n the part of Mignon, Mlle. Van Zandt has charm as an actress and virtuosity as a singer. Her childlike face, with two big astonished untroubled eyes, her relaxed attitude and her feminine grace win the audience at once; the exquisite finesse and the suppleness of her voice do the rest.[51]
>
> I ask the Opéra-Comique and Mlle. Van Zandt permission to give them only one "bravo" at this point; as the theatre and the charming singer have finally exhausted praise. To whom would I have something new to say about the success of *Mignon*, renewed with the charm of Mlle. Van Zandt, with the tender and penetrating accents of her voice, the pure and harmonious breath with which she sings? It is Lakmé and Mignon together, both the dream-child of poets, the poetry detached from the earth and taken up to the heavens.[52]

They also praised her for her performance in *Lakmé*:

> As for the interpretation, it is always excellent. The Opéra-Comique audience gave a veritable ovation for the charming Mlle. Van Zandt, for a superb performance in the role of Lakmé. She has childlike charm and grace which embodies the character. The unusual silvery timbre of her voice, her prodigious virtuosity, her original style, are special gifts that complete the theatrical illusion and set her apart from other singers of the day.[53]

Marie's clipping folders, which her family has preserved, contain many articles full of similarly unalloyed praise for her performances during this period. However, her "spoiled-child" reputation persisted:

> Marie Van Zandt debuted in the role of Mignon, and everyone knows how successful that was. Almost immediately the vivacious American became the spoiled child of the Opéra-Comique public. "Spoiled child" is

the right term. Mlle. Van Zandt has the qualities and the faults of spoiled children. She is nice, a bit bizarre, attractive but sometimes a bit more capricious than called for. It is not only with her director that she sometimes takes somewhat cavalier liberties, it is also with the music…She is something of an exaggerated fantasy; in sum, she is an interesting personality. The Opéra-Comique public is delicate and refined; if it is so fond of Mlle. Van Zandt, it is because she has qualities above and beyond the ordinary.

Whatever one makes of it, in returning in *Mignon* Mlle. Van Zandt has given an act of taste and remembrance. Mignon is, with Dinorah in the *Pardon of Ploermel*, her best role. It is especially in the second act, the best part of the score, that the diva displays the best of her personal qualities. She plays with much mischievous grace the cross-dressing scene and becomes very touching in the farewell scene that follows it. She received a splendid ovation at the end of the second act and at the end of the opera. Soon she will return to us in *Lakmé*. In spite of her faults it is always a delight to see her again.[54]

Marie continued singing at the Opéra-Comique until late June, and her name appeared often in Paris newspapers during the spring and summer of 1884—including a very flattering analysis of her handwriting.[55] *Le Figaro* reported that she sang at a "very brilliant" soirée on May 22 at the Japanese embassy, attended by two hundred fifty of "the grandest names in Parisian society"; she was "truly prodigious. She shared the success of the soirée with M. Braga, the eminent cellist."[56] On May 24, *Le Figaro* announced that Marie would sing two pieces, including "Les Enfants" with Massenet at the piano, as part of a May 31 retirement tribute to Jules Pasdeloup, a conductor and major figure on the Parisian music scene.[57]

Minor Stumbles

In early May 1884, an incident occurred that threatened to tarnish Marie's glittering artistic and public reputation. On May 7 and 8, a number of Paris newspapers printed almost identical brief stories saying that Marie had sued an American reporter, J. H. Haynie, for stories in the Boston *Herald* and the San Francisco *Chronicle*. Marie claimed that these stories (which we have not been able to access) "attacked her dignity as a woman and an artist" by accusing her of being responsible for the well-known American soprano Emma Nevada's departure from the Opéra-Comique. The case was scheduled for hearing on May 15,[58] but we could find no report of how it was resolved. In any event, Nevada left Paris around this time to tour America with J. H. Mapleson's opera company, and the issue was apparently forgotten.

A potentially more serious stumble, involving the highest levels of British royalty, occurred soon after this. Following her hugely successful season in France, Marie vacationed in England in July and early August. During this stay, she was invited to a dinner attended by the Princess of Wales, but for some reason she did not appear. A July 11 letter to Marie from Charlotte Knollys, the princess's private secretary (and her Lady of the Bedchamber when the princess became queen consort to Edward VII), indicates that Marie had written to her expressing concern about offending the princess (fig. 15):

Dear Miss Van Zandt,
  I can assure you that it is quite a mistake about the Princess being displeased at your not coming to Lady Mandeville's the evening she dined there. Her Royal Highness would certainly have had great pleasure in hearing you sing but at the same time perfectly understood the reasons which prevented you doing so on that particular occasion.
  Hoping that the above explanation will relieve your mind from all fear of having given offense…[59]

It would be very interesting to know what reasons Marie gave, but we could find no information about the incident in her papers or in a search of French and British newspaper archives. An August 4 letter to Marie from Lady Emily Peel, daughter-in-law of former Prime Minister Robert Peel, indicates that Marie did visit the prince and princess later in July but was concerned about being the subject of adverse rumors (fig. 16):

Dear Mlle. Van Zandt,
  Thanks for sending me Miss Knollys' letter. I had a long talk with the Prince and Princess of Wales about you after you left and the

Prince was most kind about you. There is no doubt about your getting the letter you want and if you have not received it by the time you require it write me a line and I will see to it. Nothing could exceed both the Prince's and Princess's kindness to me in this matter and she entered fully into the various rumours, which she said had no foundation. In any case she was pleased she said to do anything of use…[60]

There is no letter from the Prince or Princess of Wales in her papers, and we do not know what rumors were of concern at this time. In any case, these gracious replies show that Marie remained in high regard in the highest levels of English society despite her apparent snub of a royal invitation.

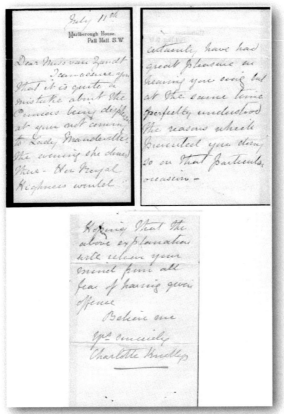

Figure 15. Letter to Marie from Charlotte Knollys, private secretary to the Princess of Wales, July 11, 1884.

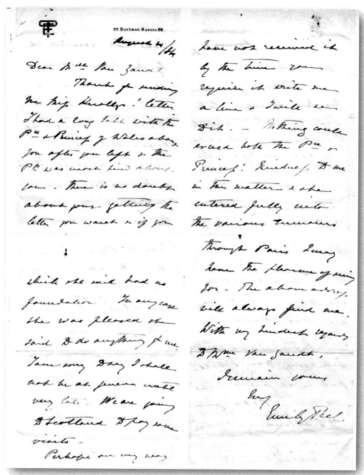

Figure 16. Letter to Marie from Lady Emily Peel, daughter-in-law of former Prime Minister Robert Peel, August 4, 1884.

A Major Stumble

A much more serious incident occurred at the Opéra-Comique about three months later. Marie was cast as Rosina in Rossini's *The Barber of Seville*. This was a new role for her, in Italian, and her earlier tutor Francesco Lamperti was summoned from Milan to coach her. Her anxiety at playing this new and difficult role was reported in *Le Figaro*:

The truth is that Van Zandt has, like all worthy artists, the honorable fault of self-doubt and is suffering great qualms. That Italian music generates those; the rhymes seem difficult to her and less easily grasped than she is used to…Naturally, she told [Lamperti] of her fears about the part of Rosina. The old master told her…that "you are the most delicious of Rosinas."…Thus the student worked dutifully on the part and, as Lamperti is the most faithful guardian of Rossinian traditions, the role will be in good hands.[61]

On the opening night, November 8, Marie performed perfectly in her brief appearance in the first act. Rosina has the major role in the second act, which includes the "singing-lesson" scene, in which she was to sing a piece of her own composition. But when Marie came on stage, she staggered, her voice failed, and she could not continue. The audience was furious, and Marie was hissed and accused of being drunk. Interestingly—and suspiciously—Cécile Mézéray, an Opéra-Comique soprano who had played Rosina, was in the audience and volunteered to assume the role: "[T]he self-righteous Gounod [composer of the opera *Faust*] hardly helped matters by personally leading Cécile Mézéray onstage in mid-performance to replace the unfortunate American."[62] Thus the opera eventually continued, but Marie was left nearly alone and desolated in her dressing room.

This incident was the talk of Paris the next day. Marie was clearly severely affected, at least psychologically:

The diva, who was allowed to remain up for about two hours, could only receive a few visitors, among whom was Ambroise Thomas [the composer of *Mignon*]. Many of the callers of distinction left their calling cards, among them the Grand Duke Vladimir [uncle of the last tsar and a well-known international patron of the arts]. As soon as the diva feels a bit stronger, she will spend a few days at Versailles or Fontainebleau to recuperate completely and…get away from the Parisian curiosity which continues to be a menace to the invasion of her privacy.[63]

To protect her reputation, Marie immediately wrote a letter to the editor of *Le Soleil* saying that

> I appeal to your good will to help me put an end to the deplorable error of which I am the victim. I was seized on the stage yesterday at the moment of beginning my big aria with a physical indisposition which, added to apprehensions that all artists will understand, in starting a new part on the stage of the Opéra-Comique…The doctor of the theatre, and Mr. Carvalho can affirm…that it is to that cause that my faltering was attributed…I affirm again that at the moment that I began my aria…I was a prey of such vertigo that I lost the sense of all that was going on around me.[64]

On November 12, *Le Soleil*'s editor published his own letter supporting Marie's explanation, saying that "M. Carvalho declared that [four] doctors consulted individually by him have also declared that…she was the prey to vertigo…" However, his letter added to the controversy by concluding with

> Let us add that during the day Mlle. Van Zandt had used a medicine, basically phosphorus, without paying attention to the dose prescribed by her doctor. Mr. Carvalho confirms that another artist…having once used the same medicine had felt the same effect.[65]

Marie had not given that explanation for her indisposition, and her doctor, Dr. Love, responded with a letter that gave the prescription, stated that it was in widespread use, and concluded that "it is not to [this] medicine that one must attribute the sudden and prolonged indisposition of which [Mlle. Van Zandt] has been the unfortunate victim."[66]

The idea that she had taken too large a dose of Dr. Love's medicine persisted in some accounts and was later affirmed by her mother. However, there were many who thought that Marie had been drugged by one or more rivals, and this theory was supported in articles that appeared long after the incident. In 1907, Marie's father stated that

The demonstration against my daughter was brought about through the objections of some of the artists of that theater to having Miss Van Zandt appear so constantly while they were, as they thought, unnecessarily kept in the background...Mr. Carvalho, the director... responded that the box office gave the best reason why Mlle. Van Zandt was so frequently singing.[67]

While this explanation might be thought to reflect a father's bias, a more contemporary article by a member of the Opéra-Comique orchestra does suggest a plot by a rival, not Cécile Mézéray but a Mlle. Adler, who had been playing Lakmé in Marie's absence:

[C]ertain newspapers...speak of a cabal; the fanatics of Mlle. Adler, furious...to see their favorite dispossessed of a part that she had played so long that she considered it her property, wanted to protest.[68]

Another, much later, clipping provides dark details of such a cabal involving Marie's backstage maid, although the perpetrator is not named:

Some two years after that memorable event, this maid was taken seriously ill and placed in a hospital...where she died. A few days before that she revealed to her nurse, a nun, ...her participation in the act which produced that incident. She stated that she was approached by a person who paid her a large sum to drug the orange water which Marie was in the habit of sipping during her operatic performances.[69]

Given the above newspaper report of her anxiety about her debut in *Barber* and her own contemporary testimony, it seems likely that her stumble was simply a case of stage fright. However, the possibility that Marie was a victim of a rival's tampering with her doctor's phosphorus potion cannot be ruled out, especially given the presence of a ready substitute, Cécile Mézéray, in the audience. Whatever the cause, the treatment of Marie in this incident engendered some strong anti-French sentiments in American and English newspapers and anti-American feelings in French newspapers, and as we will see, the controversy shadowed Marie for decades.

In any case, Marie quit the Opéra-Comique, and almost immediately after the *Barber of Seville* incident, she and her mother left Paris for Saint Petersburg, where Marie had previously contracted to sing for the 1884–85 season.

CHAPTER 7

A Turbulent Year: Russia, Paris, and England, 1884–85

THE TURMOIL RESULTING FROM THE *Barber of Seville* incident did not follow Marie to Saint Petersburg, where she continued to be adored by audiences and was a great favorite of the Russian court. However, Director Carvalho was concerned about the reception she would receive from the Parisian public when she returned to the Opéra-Comique in the spring of 1885. To assure her a warm welcome, he made the tickets for her first performance—*Lakmé*—available mostly to wealthy admirers of hers, and had police on hand to quell any disturbance. Ordinary Parisian opera-goers resented this, and some whistling and hissing were heard during the first three performances. On the night of the fourth performance, the discontent erupted into a riot and Marie had to escape from the theater by a back door. The next day, she wrote a public letter to Carvalho asking to be released from her contract, and she did not sing again in Paris until 1896. However, these incidents did not affect her confidence or her acclaim in the rest of Europe, and she returned to London in the summer of 1885 for a very successful series of operatic appearances. And, although she once again apparently snubbed a royal invitation, she continued to be a favorite of the highest levels of English society, and concluded that summer with a concert at Buckingham Palace. A turbulent year indeed!

ACCLAIM IN SAINT PETERSBURG
Marie was singing in Saint Petersburg within a month after leaving Paris. On December 9, 1884, she wrote a letter from the Grand Hôtel d'Europe in that city conveying birthday greetings to her brother "Tonie" and reporting, "My

success here has been tremendous. They say that since Patti such enthusiasm has not been witnessed" (fig. 17). This letter—the only one we have in Marie's handwriting—was signed "Wissie v. Z." and has a PS saying "We are almost sure to be in America next year." This is one of several false alarms about Marie's making an American tour, which actually did not occur until late 1891.

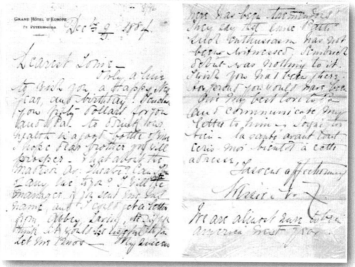

Figure 17. Letter from Marie to her brother "Tonie," December 9, 1884.

Marie spent the rest of the 1884–85 season in Saint Petersburg, where she was the darling of the court and showed again her remarkable ability for learning new material by singing *Lakmé* in Italian instead of the original French. On December 21, 1884, an English-language newspaper, datelined Paris, reported that

> It will be remembered that Mlle. Van Zandt was a short time ago the victim of a mean calumny on the part of certain newspapers. Since then she has gone to St. Petersburg in performance of a temporary engagement. It was expected that the Russian public would avenge the want of courtesy shown here towards this charming and talented singer, and this expectation has been amply realized. A telegram from St. Petersburg announces that Mlle. Van Zandt has made her debut there, that the Emperor [Tsar], the Empress, and the whole Court

were present, and that the enthusiasm which she evoked exceeded anything seen for years. Mlle. Van Zandt was recalled 30 times.[70]

She made her farewell appearance in Saint Petersburg on March 7, 1885. A special dispatch to the *New York Herald* reported that this was "a veritable triumph," also eliciting thirty recalls. In addition,

> A beautiful American flag was handed up to the stage as one of the tributes to the singer. Over 800 wreaths were showered upon the stage, beside the many costly presents that were carried up. All the members of the imperial family were present.[71]

A souvenir of this visit to Russia is a silver vase, inscribed to "Marie Van Zandt from her friends Yuri and Popov, Pages to the Emperor, 1885" (fig. 18). During this stay, Marie met and was courted by Grand Duke Mikhail Mikhailovich, second cousin to the tsar, as described in chapter 9.

Figure 18. Silver vase given to Marie in Saint Petersburg, inscribed to "Marie Van Zandt from her friends Yuri and Popov, Pages to the Emperor, 1885." Courtesy of Susan L. [Van Zandt] Ferraro.

A Troubled Return and Farewell to Paris

Marie then returned to Paris to resume her career at the Opéra-Comique. Director Carvalho considered Marie his protégé and wanted to provide an opportunity for her to erase the memories of the *Barber of Seville* incident of the previous November and to reestablish her as a star of his theater. He chose *Lakmé* as the best vehicle to do this, and the first performance was on March 18, 1885—only ten days after her return from Russia.

Marie was understandably anxious about how the Paris audience would receive her, and so was Carvalho. In fact, Carvalho had arranged for a substantial police presence to assure that no disturbance would occur. He had also arranged for all the tickets for the first performance to be bought up by "a gentle singer" (probably Adelina Patti) and "a famous banker" (probably Adolphe Rothschild) and, through them, made available only to people who would be sympathetic to Marie.[72] As a result,

> The occasion might have been mistaken for a *première*, and that of the first order, judging from the superb toilettes and glittering diamonds seen in almost every part of the house…Mlle. Van Zandt…found herself in the presence of the whole American colony, the leading theatre-goers of the capital, its entire press, and the correspondents of all the chief newspapers of the globe.[73]

There was some disturbance outside the theater before the show, as ordinary French patrons hoping to get tickets found them sold out. There were also the beginnings of a disturbance in the theater, in spite of Carvalho's precautions.[74] Thus Marie had good reason to be anxious. However, she quickly overcame her fears to deliver a strong performance:

> As soon as the curtain rose, the prayer of the Goddess Shiva rises above the great chorus, started in the depths of the set by Lakmé, who approaches little by little, enters on the stage, and comes to finish her song in front of the footlights. The voice of Mlle. Van Zandt trembled very much during the first measures, when the young singer could

not yet see the orchestra seats in which she feared to meet her severe critics…Courage returned to her when she was face to face with them. The last note of the prayer was followed by a short silence, so short that anxiety did not have time to arise. A few timid signs of applause came from the balcony, these were echoed in the orchestra seats, then by a Rossinian crescendo which then changed to a unison à la Verdi. Several sly noises of protestation…faded without resistance, and no one tried to repeat them.

Peace was restored, and the visible emotion of Mlle. Van Zandt showed how much the approval of the Parisian public means to her; the most courteous, the most just, and the least rancorous in the world.[75]

The voice of Mlle. Van Zandt is, like her acting, noticeably larger, without losing either its crystalline purity in the high notes or its exquisite quality of vocalization. She reached, with her accustomed perfection, the *piquée* notes of the Bell Song in the second act; but that which I think signifies most is the dramatic accent that she gave to the same vocalizations when they were repeated, touched with sadness…Mlle. Van Zandt has made an exquisite poem of it with unaffected and deep tenderness. She was recalled at the end by long acclamations.[76]

The *Times of London* had a similar account of the evening, concluding with:

Mlle. Van Zandt exhibited…qualities of style, grace, and strength which surprised even her admirers. She gave the last measures with a spirit and amplitude which brought to a climax the enthusiasm of the spectators…It is to be hoped this evening will put an end to an unfortunate misunderstanding and that henceforth this singer will again become the *enfant gatée* [spoiled child] of the Parisian public.[77]

However, the first performance of her return did not put an end to the public's agitation, and an undercurrent of discontent continued. Tickets to the general public remained restricted, and the police presence was maintained at the second performance on March 20. Perhaps in part because of this, whistling was heard as soon as Marie began to sing, but there was an uproar in the audience protesting the whistlers. At this the curtain was closed, and at the behest of Carvalho, a police official stepped onto the stage and asked the audience if they wanted the performance to proceed. The response was *"oui, oui,"* and the opera resumed and concluded, with Marie receiving much applause and several curtain calls.

A similar incident took place at the third performance, on March 23:

> Outside, before: Several youths, who were in line but were not able to get tickets, made a disturbance…This required…the Commissioner of Police to give the order to take one of them to the police station to restore order.
>
> Inside, after: *Lakmé* began 20 minutes late. Mlle. Van Zandt appeared…She sang her duet with Mlle. Dupont. People applauded. But, in the middle of the bravos, two or three sharp whistles were heard. The public and the orchestra rose as one person and applauded fiercely, shouting "Throw the whistlers out!"…Mlle. Van Zandt and Mlle. Dupont, holding on to each other, impassively observed the scene in front of them: this curious spectacle of an audience that turned its back on them to defend them and to shout down the whistlers. Finally, things quieted down, and to prove to the two singers that everyone is on their side, they were asked to continue their duet. The rest of the performance was nothing but a long ovation for Mlle. Van Zandt and M. Degenne.[78]

At the fourth performance, on March 26, the discontent erupted into a riot. *Le Figaro* reported that

> A note appeared yesterday evening in a newspaper revealing a hostile attitude on the part of M. Carvalho…[P]eople prepared for war, the whistlers booked tickets…Yesterday, at 7:00 PM, there was a long line

at the…box office.…There was a notice: "Because of pre-sale of tickets, only a limited number are available." This note naturally irritated the public. "The trick is obvious," said people in line, largely young people aged 18 to 25. "M. Carvalho has given all the tickets to his cronies…It's a shame that the director of a publicly subsidized theatre should behave like this. That man must be fired." Others said the opposite: "Carvalho and Rothschild are protecting Van Zandt."

At 7:45 the box office opened, but closed soon after. There were no more tickets. At this news, the protests got louder…People whistled. Someone cried "Down with Carvalho." The mob gathered and blocked traffic. People booed at people with tickets. Finally it became real mischief. The little disturbance got big.[79]

The doors then opened, and people entered the theatre. The *Le Figaro* reporter gives a detailed description of the scene in the theater: Marie's entrance in the first scene was greeted with a mixture of applause and hisses. This happened again when she entered in scene 2. At this, "the orchestra rose and, arms in the air, they acclaimed Van Zandt." This was followed by a whistle, which was countered with furious applause. The scene was repeated when Marie entered later.

> Each time they whistle, I look at Van Zandt. She is very calm. Never has she sung better. Then, when the hisses redoubled, she folded her arms and became tense. There was a nervous movement which made one think that she felt ill. The orchestra started up again. People called "encore, encore." She began again, but this time it was hisses from one end to the other. After [the next scene], the curtain fell…I tried to determine the number of hecklers. I would guess scarcely more than 20, but they had very loud whistles.[80]

In spite of the disturbances, which were repeated in the second and third acts and included breaking down a gate protecting the stage door and the arrest of two young men, the opera was performed to the end.

After the fall of the curtain, Mlle. Van Zandt appears twice, very emotional, with her hand over her heart. The entire room is standing. People wave their hats and shout "Bravo! Bravo!" But hisses continue. People leave saying "That's the last of *Lakmé*."…The mob outside the stage door waits for Mlle. Van Zandt, some to acclaim her, some to boo her. But she leaves by a back door.[81]

A substantial portion of the front page of *Le Figaro* of March 28 was devoted to the incidents of the preceding days, including a lengthy "Paris Courier" column by Albert Wolff chastising the youth who created the disturbances, a letter from "A Member of the American Colony," and a long interview with Marie by "Charles". Wolff's column contrasted at length the bloody French defeat in Indochina, news of which was just reaching Paris, with the frivolous protests of Marie by Parisian youth:

All day, the roads of Tonkin strewn with French bodies…; the field of battle abandoned by the brave General Négrier, but the Opéra-Comique gloriously overrun by whistlers. Far away, the sadness of a bloody defeat; here the joy of having finally conquered a young artist. Some might say the comparison was rather meager.[82]

The American's letter concluded with

[W]e other Americans are not able to bear the belief that our young compatriot merits the hostility that part of the public directed at her, given that French artists always find a most favorable welcome in the United States.[83]

Charles's interview provides interesting insight into twenty-three-year-old Marie's state of mind—very affected by the ordeal, but mature and confident:

About four o'clock I presented myself at Mlle. Van Zandt's home, which occupies, with her family, a lovely second story at 4 rue Christoph Colomb—a true American street. She extended her hand to me. "Well," I asked her, "are you recovered?" She was full of smiles, but very pale, with blue circles around her eyes. "What an evening," she cooed in a pretty Franco-American sing-song. "I almost lost courage. Truly, people did everything they could to console me. As you see." The apartment is full of flowers. On the carpet, behind a folding screen, there was an immense, but elegant, wheelbarrow containing bunches of white lilacs.

"And I have received many letters and messages. These are especially from French and Russians, who have flattered me." "Have you exactly defined the emotion you felt yesterday?" "Oh, perfectly…It is to be better than ever. Not for an instant had I lost composure. I hoped, I swear it, that the whistlers would calm down. I counted on the pretty tune of "The Clochette." I have sung it often in Russia. I sing it now exactly as I feel. Yesterday, I took it to my heart, to my soul. You noticed? It is so beautiful."

Here, she sang it. Yes, I had the pleasure to have a piece from *Lakmé* for myself alone…At the end she interrupted herself brusquely with a whistle and a gesture of a despairing child. "I did all I could to win over those who wished me ill, and then—Xiii, Xiii—oh, it was truly frightening."[84]

Marie's reappearance at the Opéra-Comique and her demeanor during all the disturbances clearly demonstrated her spirit and talent and her regard for the Parisian public, and it seemed she had reestablished herself in the good graces of the great majority of that public. She was quoted as saying, "I believe the ringleaders had been bribed to whistle and hiss, and I made up my mind to remember that I was an American girl and to show American pluck."[85]

Indeed, the disturbances were something of an international incident, and the *New York Times* of March 28 reported that

Marie Van Zandt…said the wanton attacks that had been made upon her had so affected her nervous system that for a number of nights she could not sleep. The plaudits and kindness of her audiences had however consoled her for the injustice of the insults which had been offered by the clique which persecuted her. Miss Van Zandt said she hoped to sing in Paris, but it would not be for years hence. A number of letters from Americans appear in the *Figaro* protesting against the treatment to which Miss Van Zandt has been subjected and expressing surprise that the press of Paris was not unanimous in denouncing the torture inflicted on the young American artiste when they are aware that the French are always favorably received in America. A number of students who are indignant at the insults heaped upon the American singer have sent a petition to the Minister of the Interior praying that the free admission of journalists into subsidized theaters be forbidden, as, the petition states, they keep a paying public freezing outside.[86]

The pretext for the disturbances of March 18–26, 1885, was Marie's faltering in the *Barber of Seville* the previous November, the true cause of which is not clear. As we have seen, Marie herself claimed to have suffered vertigo due to stage fright because of singing a difficult new role, while Carvalho and her doctors claimed she had drunk too much of a prescribed potion. There is also reason to suspect that the potion was spiked by one or more jealous colleagues.

In any case, the incident provided an excuse for elements of the public to turn against her, perhaps because they felt that this young American was being favored over French singers. One contemporary account quoted a man as saying he had heckled Marie because he had recently read that she had insulted France.[87] However, the newspaper reports cited above, and others, suggest that the disruptions were in large part directed at Carvalho who, in his attempt to assure a warm reception for Marie's return to the Opéra-Comique, had most of the tickets bought up and made available only to her supporters, excluding the usual opera-going public. The large police presence may also have been provocative.

But the reason for the large disturbance at the fourth performance on March 26 may have had little to do with Marie or Carvalho. The Sino-French war was raging at this time, and news had just reached Paris announcing a defeat and retreat of the French army at Lang Son, Viet Nam. This triggered a major political crisis, known as the "Lang Son Affair," which ultimately resulted in Prime Minister Jules Ferry's resignation on March 30. Some people thought that the theater disturbance was allowed, and perhaps encouraged, by officials to distract from Lang Son, and an observer on the scene on March 26 reported, "I heard this frightening comment: 'The government has a defeat in China, but a victory at the Opéra-Comique.'"[88] This explanation was corroborated years later by M. Goron, who was a junior police officer during this period but later became Paris's Chief of Police. In his 1897 memoir, Goron clearly stated that the police diverted demonstrators who were angry over the defeat at Lang Son to vent their anger at the Opéra-Comique rather than at Prime Minister Ferry:

> [I] admired the way in which the police knew how to deal with the animosity of Parisians. All day the police were worried, not for Van Zandt, whom they hardly thought about, but for [Prime Minister] Jules Ferry, whom they knew was threatened by a tumultuous demonstration.
>
> The news of the retreat at Lang Son was spreading in Paris since the morning and produced enormous feeling in the population. One feared a riot, and took the most detailed precautions to guard the Prime Minister. For several days…protests against Mlle. Van Zandt occurred at the Opéra-Comique…
>
> How all of a sudden did the demonstration that left the Rue Montmartre to find M. Ferry find itself at the Opéra-Comique?… Someone cried "There is Van Zandt!" The crowd rushed forward. [A scuffle] went on until it was too late for the demonstrators to go to Ferry's office. It is thus that the last victim of Lang Son was poor Mlle. Van Zandt…[89]

This story was repeated by the *New York Times*, showing that both the French and American public maintained an interest in Marie's life and career for more than a decade after the incident:

> M. Goron…declares that the memorable and offensive attack upon [Miss Van Zandt] was engineered by the followers of M. Ferry to counteract an intended demonstration against him by Radicals and Socialists after the disastrous defeat of the French at Lang Son.

M. Camescasse, the Prefect of Police of the day, was consulted as to how to prevent the intended demonstration against the unpopular M. Ferry and, according to M. Goron, he suggested a monster demonstration against Miss Van Zandt. All the available detectives and theatrical claques were sent to the Opéra-Comique to howl at and hiss the American singer.

Whenever there was lull in the uproar the cry was raised that Miss Van Zandt was going out by another door, and so successful was the trick that the excitement was maintained until midnight, and the attention of the intending anti-Ferry demonstrators was diverted until it was too late to go to the foreign office.[90]

Included in the *Le Figaro* interview was the letter Marie had just written to Carvalho asking to be released immediately from her Opéra-Comique contract, which was due to end on May 31:

My Dear M. Carvalho,

If I could only count on the courtesy of the public, I would not hesitate to continue my performances.

As my presence at the Opéra-Comique has provoked outside disturbances, my right as a foreigner is to again ask you to release me from the contract with your theatre.

No one dares impose on an artist the obligation to confront one more time the emotions which I have just encountered. I leave your theatre with a profound understanding that the true public continues to lavish encouragement on me and that the great majority of the press has protested against the injustice made to an artist, and against the injury done to a woman.

The acclamations that have greeted me during these recent ordeals greatly console me from the cabal organized against me, and I carry the conviction that the public will render justice to me.

Believe, my dear director, in the affectionate devotion of your grateful

Marie Van Zandt[91]

She told the interviewer that "I will return when all is forgotten," and asked him, "Do you think that will take more than two years?" He replied, "Oh… not even." But she did not give a public performance again in Paris until 1896.

Stardom and Snubs of Royalty in England

On the eve of her return to the Paris stage in 1896, Marie told an interviewer that

> On leaving [Paris], almost 12 years ago, I was very sad and very sick. The next two years I was terribly nervous; at the least word about music, the name "barber" popping up in conversation, hearing an operatic melody, made me sick all over again. Only after two years was I able to calm myself.[92]

This seems belied by the fact that, only two months after the calamitous incidents at the Opéra-Comique, she returned to London to a very successful series of appearances in *Lakmé, Mignon,* and *Mireille* as part of a "13th Season of French Plays" at the Gaiety Theatre under the management of M. L. Mayer (fig. 19). As in her London debut six years earlier, these performances were very well received:

> Miss Van Zandt comes to us now with perfected talent and a great reputation; and she achieved on Saturday night [June 6th] in the part of Lakmé such a success as is obtained on the operatic stage perhaps half a dozen times in the course of a century…[O]ne must go back twenty-four years to the first appearance in London of Adelina Patti… for a parallel performance to that of Miss Van Zandt…[Her] voice is exceptionally high, and its quality is exceptionally fine. Her very highest notes, too, are wonderfully soft and delicate; and she reaches altitudes that are quite beyond the reach of other singers…She sings in any case—in the most rapid and difficult flights as in passages of more measured character—absolutely in time. She is a perfect actress, moreover; and the play of her countenance, her gestures, and her attitudes are all admirably expressive.[93]

[A]fter the first reception of the new prima donna, as the opera proceeded the enthusiasm of the audience knew no bounds, and again and again, in the midst of recalls…offerings of flowers were thrown or handed upon the stage…It is long since so remarkable a voice has been heard in London. Fresh, pure, trilling, of excellent compass, and with a clear resonance in the long-drawn deliciously sustained high notes, there is something almost birdlike in some of the passages, while the ease with which these effects are produced is wonderful. When to such a voice is joined youth, an agreeable appearance, and good histrionic power, it is no wonder that there should be such a furor as greeted Mlle. Van Zandt…Mlle. Van Zandt's acting and singing throughout the opera were beyond praise…[94]

The assumption of the title role in *Mignon* by Mlle. Van Zandt was a complete success…[She] realizes the portrait to perfection.[95]

Figure 19. (a) Card announcing the 1885 summer season of opera and French plays at London's Gaiety Theatre; (b) card announcing Marie's summer 1885 appearances in *Lakmé*, *Mignon*, and *Mireille* at London's Gaiety Theatre.

Clearly, the English opera-going public considered Marie a star of the first rank, and her treatment by the Parisian audience in March was still very much on their minds. This, and the very high regard in which she was held by English society and the musical elite, are made clear in a May 26 letter to Marie from Sir Arthur Sullivan, composer of the Gilbert and Sullivan operettas and other works, when he seems to refer to Marie's July 1884 "snub" of the Prince of Wales (fig. 20):

> My dear Marie,
> You gave me such a snub last year, when I asked you to meet the Prince of Wales here, that I have considerable hesitation in asking such a thing again. But I have a small and *very select* party for the Prince here on Sunday June 7th...His Royal Highness expresses a strong wish to meet you to hear you sing here on that evening. So, undeterred by former defeat, I again try to get you to my humble little dwelling. Will you come and help me with my music that evening? The people you will find here are the crème de la crème of London society, all anxious to welcome you heartily; all eager to prove to you by the warmth of their reception in what horror and disgust they hold the brutal and cowardly treatment you have been subjected to. My poochie, my heart bled for you, as I told you in my letter at the time, and I longed to be at the head of a battery of artillery to sweep that scum clean off to—well Hades. The Prince says "Miss Van Zandt arrives on the 6th," so he knows all your movements... Write me a note and say "Yes, I'll come"...Give my love to your mother, and with much to yourself, believe me dear Marie..."

This letter seems to imply that turning down this second invitation would be taken *very* seriously. This was awkward because, as shown in figure 19, Marie was scheduled to perform *Lakmé* on June 6 and 9 at the Gaiety. Manager Mayer must have objected to her singing for the prince on the seventh, because a June 2 letter from Sullivan (fig. 21) says

> I saw Mr. Mayer today and did my best to combat his objections to your coming here next Sunday [June 7th]. He has promised to let

me know…tomorrow. Since then I have seen Mr. Francis Knollys [Private Secretary to the Prince of Wales], who says that the Prince of Wales takes a strong personal interest in your coming here, and he expressed himself *very strongly* about anyone trying to forbid you to accept an…invitation which does not interfere with your professional occupation. I fear there will be grave dissatisfaction if Mr. Mayer tries to prevent your coming and his Royal Highness's strong personal interest in you and warm good feeling towards Mr. Mayer's undertaking may receive a severe check. Try and induce Mayer to give his approval graciously.

In spite of these very strong words, it appears that Marie did not accept the prince's invitation, possibly because Mayer did not release her. She (or perhaps her mother, as the reply is addressed to "Madam") apparently wrote to the prince giving her reasons, and his private secretary coolly acknowledged receipt of that letter on June 9 (fig. 22):

Madam,
    I am desired by the Prince of Wales to convey to you the expression of his thanks for your letter to his Royal Highness.

Soon after, an article in an English-language Paris newspaper said

Miss Marie Van Zandt is in trouble again—in disgrace this time with the Prince of Wales, because she refused to go to Sir Arthur Sullivan's dinner party to meet his Royal Highness and some other proper gentlemen. She gives as her excuse that she had a dinner *chez elle* that same evening, and that several French authors and artistes were to be her guests. Now that the little American has shown her preferences for French *littèrateurs* over the first gentleman of Great Britain, perhaps Paris will forgive her and welcome her back again.[96]

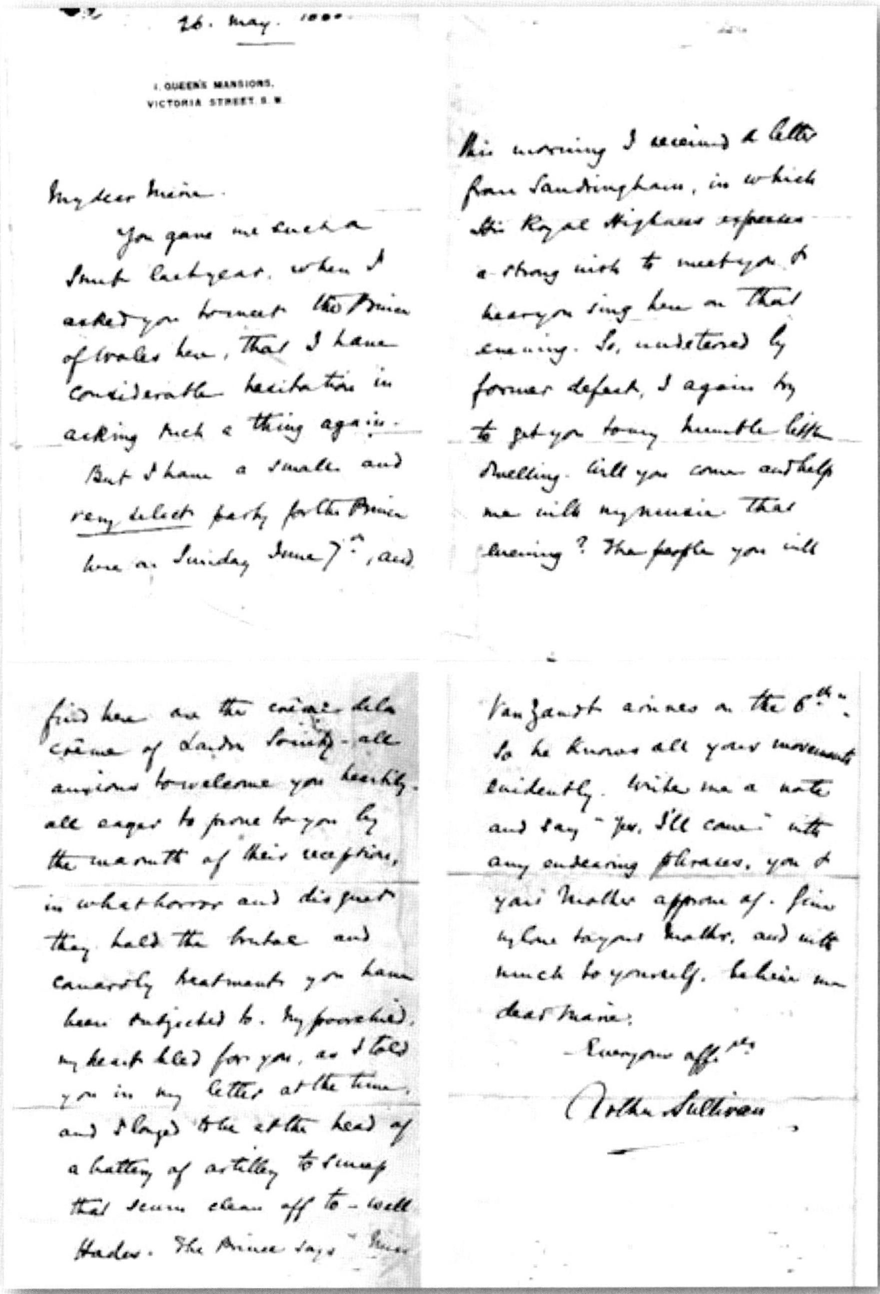

Figure 20. Letter to Marie from Sir Arthur Sullivan, May 26, 1885.

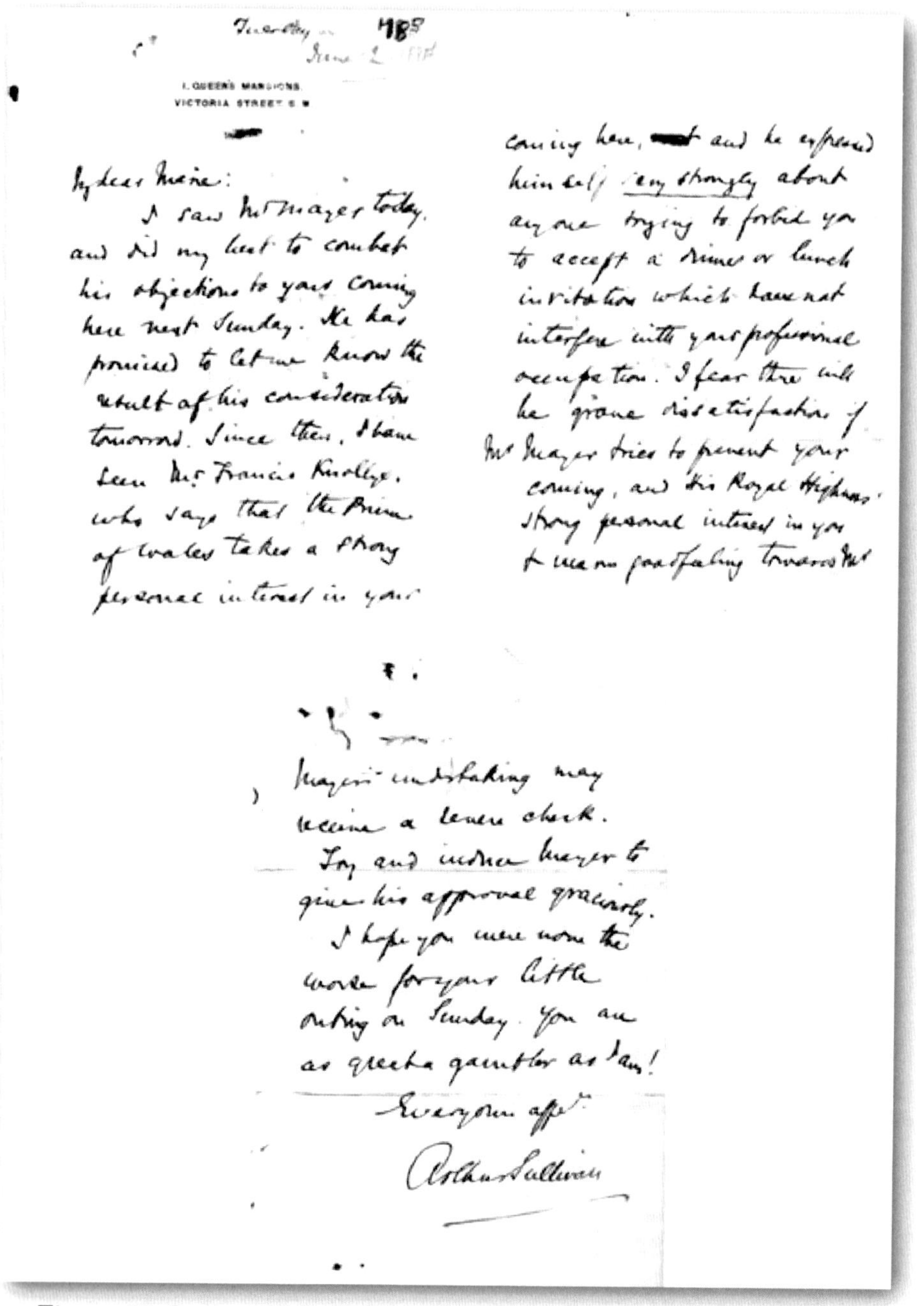

Figure 21. Letter to Marie from Sir Arthur Sullivan, June 2, 1885.

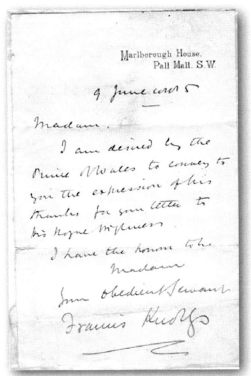

Figure 22. Letter to Marie, or perhaps her mother, from Francis Knollys, private secretary to the Prince of Wales, June 9, 1885.

Meanwhile, Jennie invited Adelina Patti, who was back in London to sing *Carmen*, to meet with her and Marie. Miss Patti replied from the Midland Hotel on June 24 (fig. 23):

My dear friend,
   Thanks for your card. I shall be most pleased to see you and dear Marie on Sunday as on Thursday I rehearse "Carmen."

Marie's charm and renown must have overcome her apparent disgrace for twice seriously snubbing the Prince of Wales, because she was part of a musical soirée at Buckingham Palace a week later, in which she sang a solo and a duet (fig. 24).

Marie's engagement at the Gaiety extended through July. In September and early October, she vacationed with her mother on the Isle of Jersey and nearby Granville. *Le Figaro* reported that Marie was engaged to appear during the coming winter in twelve concerts and twelve operatic performances in Saint Petersburg (for a fee of 5,000 francs per show), as well as in Scandinavia. She left Paris for Russia on October 19.[97]

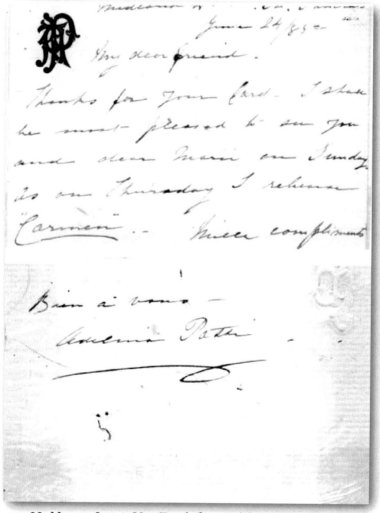

Figure 23. Note to Jennie Van Zandt from Adelina Patti, June 24, 1885.

Figure 24. Program for a Buckingham Palace soirée, July 3, 1885.

CHAPTER 8

Return to Russia, Illness, and Recuperation, 1886

IN THE WINTER OF 1885–86, Marie sang in Saint Petersburg, then went to Moscow to sing *Lakmé*, *Barber of Seville*, *Mignon*, *The Pardon of Ploermal*, and a new leading role in Meyerbeer's *Star of the North*. On January 4, 1886, she was reported to be unable to sing because of a serious cold.[98] Marie became seriously ill in early March; on March 7, Adolphe Blowitz, the well-known Paris correspondent of the *London Times*, wrote to her (presumably in Saint Petersburg), "You can easily imagine how great must be my anxiety to know that you are sick, far from this Paris where you felt so well and where so many hearts remain faithful to you." Two weeks later, *Le Figaro* reported that

> Marie Van Zandt has fallen dangerously ill in St. Petersburg. However, the latest news is better. As soon as she is able to travel, she will go to Cannes for a few days. We hope she will make a full recovery.
> This illness has arrived at a bad time, interrupting what had begun as a marvelous season for the artist. Her success in Moscow was such that it was hoped she would be engaged for a new series of performances. After that, she was going to give performances of *Mignon* in Berlin and then make a grand series of concerts across Germany and Scandinavia. Finally, she would end her tour at Stockholm…Will she be able to complete that schedule? Probably not.[99]

By March 31 she was recuperating at a spa in Augsburg, Bavaria, with her mother and sister. Her recuperation continued through the summer, and an

August 2 letter from her father, James Rose Van Zandt, in the *New York World* explains what happened:

> Miss Van Zandt, while in Moscow last winter filling an operatic engagement, contracted a severe indisposition through singing certain portions of the opera of *Mignon* in her stocking feet. Her contract at Moscow expired a few days thereafter, and the young lady, although still suffering from cold, went to St. Petersburg to complete her engagement in that city. Her illness there increased, developing into a severe form of typhoid fever, from which, however, she has happily recovered. The disease, nevertheless, left its traces—it usually makes its "black mark"—and culminated in an attack of inflammatory rheumatism in the feet, from which, however, she was rapidly recovering when the writer of this left Europe, some three weeks since [i.e., in early July].[100]

On September 8 Marie and her mother moved to another Bavarian spa, at Wildbad, where there was a specialist who created a leg brace for her.

It was probably during their return from Germany to Paris that fall that Marie and Jennie were in Berlin and were personally invited by another of the major political figures of Europe, German Chancellor Otto von Bismarck, to dine with him (fig. 25):

> Dear Mrs. Van Zandt,
>
> In case you should choose to defer your journey for some reason or other I should be delighted if you and Miss Van Zandt would give me the honor of your company at dinner on Sunday. I will then ask a couple of friends to meet you. If you are decided to leave tomorrow night you will give me great pleasure by accepting a little lunch at the hour that is convenient for you.
>
> You will not have far to go for whilst our household is in the country I always give my little parties in the private rooms of the Kaiserhof.[101]

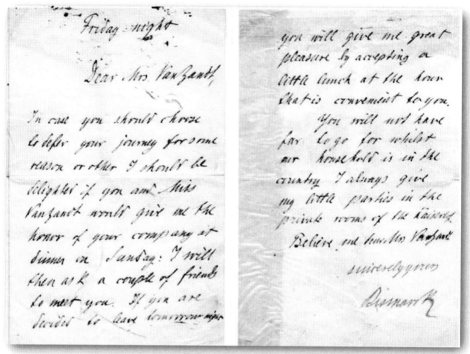

Figure 25. Undated (probably fall 1886) letter from
Otto von Bismarck to Jennie Van Zandt.

By early November they had returned to Paris, where C. Chincolle of *Le Figaro* interviewed Marie at length at her home. We give this interview virtually in its entirety, because it is quite revealing of Marie's state of mind (and finances) and of the regard in which she was viewed in France a year and a half after the turmoil at the Opéra-Comique. And, significantly, it also quotes her mother about the cause of that incident—an overdose of Dr. Love's medicine, not a plot by jealous colleagues:

> Van Zandt is in Paris! I wished since the news of her arrival to see again the poor little diva who…suffered so cruel an accident at the Opéra-Comique and who afterwards was at the point of death…
>
> Some said the artist was very ill. I thought that I was going to be introduced into her bedroom, but the door opened and to my great

surprise there was Van Zandt, standing up and smiling. She was leaning on a cane, dressed in a rose dressing gown with a black net around her neck and her golden hair piled high. I congratulated her on her pretty face, her clear blue eyes; she began to cry. The last time that I saw her was Tuesday after that terrible evening. She remembered. She fell into a chair near the fireplace.

"Do you think that they still want me?" she asked me suddenly. "If you would appear again on the stage of the Opéra-Comique you would have the greatest success of your life," I said. "Ah! I am not ready to perform!"

Her mother was there, with M. Imbert de St. Amand, the one who had presented the young artist to Madame Rothschild. We spoke of the terrible illness, so sudden, so unexpected. The poor child left Paris broken-hearted. Never could she forget the last presentation of *Lakmé*. When she thought of that scene, the memory, so burning, pained her.

She sang in Moscow, then at Saint Petersburg, always suffering. One morning she was forced to stay in bed. "It is typhoid," the doctors said. For two months she was between life and death. She suffered so that three times she tried to kill herself. Without her mother, who never ceased watching over her, it would have been the end! Later she became more cheerful, every day the emperor [Tsar], then the empress, grand dukes, or members of the highest aristocracy brought gifts; her anteroom was filled with flowers, but the doctors were afraid of the cold air of Russia, so she was taken to Wildbad. After typhoid paralysis often appears; little by little the right leg only was paralyzed. Van Zandt was taken to Augsburg where a specialist…made a walking device that held her leg right and steady. "Look—see how hard my brace is." She stretched her foot—a very tiny foot; under the red stocking are the irons which for four months have been holding her leg straight. "And does not that tire you?" "Oh, it annoys me! It is unbearable! Only, it is due to this brace that I am able now to walk 10 minutes without getting tired."

"And your voice?" I asked. "It returned also."…"Sing me your pretty Bell Song." "From *Lakmé*. Oh! I would cry if I sang it again." She already had tears in her eyes. "Well, how should I report to those who love you whether you will be able to charm them again?" She hid her face between her little hands, from which a scale burst forth. Her mother was fascinated. "Oh? Again?" she asked. We heard this time the vocalization of an octave and a half. Yes, her voice has returned, full, complete, but warmer. The voice of a woman after the voice of a child. She said, "I am now old, I am 23."

Her mother showed me the letters. From Germany and the United States, many propositions. "But where I would sing," said Van Zandt, "is where they no longer wish to hear me…" And again she recalled the incidents of the Opéra-Comique, which remain inexplicable to her.

"You see," her mother said to me, "I have been an artist myself, and so I know the situation. I have never left my child. How is it admissible that, knowing the importance of a premiere, I allowed my daughter to drink more, that day, than she was accustomed to?"

Miss Van Zandt now looked toward the sun, seeming to be dreaming. She raised her head slightly. "You know," she said, "that Mr. Delibes is half-way through *Cassya*…[Delibes never finished this opera; it was completed by Massenet after his death.]. I have always liked Mr. Delibes very much. I would have liked to be called "Cassya." But I must stay in this brace for four months. After that I will have three months of physical therapy. Therefore I will not be able to play for seven months."

A question was worrying me, just as it was all who loved Marie Van Zandt. So I allowed myself to ask "But this illness and these travels must have cost you an enormous amount of money." "Oh! Indeed they have. One doctor presented a bill for 5,000 francs. Fortunately, we do not have any worries about money. First of all, my mother is wealthy. Then I had time to earn enough not to have to sing anymore." One can recall, besides, that Mlle. Van Zandt belongs to one of the best families of the United States…

The child took from the mantle-piece an envelope from which she took a bouquet of pressed flowers. She handed me the paper that was with it: The paper, with monogrammed initials on it, had only these words: "To my little Van Zandt: to the Patti of the future. Adelina [Patti], 4th of November."

But I was afraid to tire the invalid. "Don't fear anything. I eat like four people. It is only my nerves that I would like to calm. But not to go out—that is so hard!"

She is going to stay for three weeks in Paris and then will go to Cannes where she will reside until she recovers completely. She then wanted information about the theatres. From my pocket fell an announcement of the rehearsals at the Opéra-Comique, that Saint-Saens had given me. She seized it and looked at it a long time. "Oh, Mr. Carvalho was very good to me. He knew my habits and always scheduled the rehearsals at half past one." "Well, Mademoiselle, hurry to get well and Mr. Carvalho will still be very kind to you. And all the Parisians—I can swear to it."[102]

On December 3, a Parisian English-language newspaper reported that "the favorite artist, Miss Van Zandt" had nearly recovered and is "now full of hope…and anticipates…to be able to resume a profession in which she had already won so brilliant a reputation as one of the 'Queens of Song.' Miss Van Zandt…has taken a villa at Cannes, where she will remain until spring."[103]

CHAPTER 9

Marie and Grand Duke Michael, 1885–99

IT WOULD BE NATURAL TO assume that the young, beautiful, talented, and wealthy Marie Van Zandt would have been pursued by many socially prominent male admirers. If this was the case, we have little indication of it in the materials available to us. But there are a number of records of one such admirer, Grand Duke Mikhail Mikhailovich, second cousin to Tsar Nicholas II (fig. 26). The Grand Duke, known also as Michael or Michel and to the family as "Miche-Miche" (not to be confused with the tsar's brother Michael, also a grand duke, known as "Mischa"), was born in 1861. He was a member of the Russian Imperial Court and served in the Egersky Regiment of the Guards. His good looks, generous heart, and dancing ability endeared him to Saint Petersburg society and made him a recognized favorite in the capital. At the age of twenty, after receiving his government stipend ($100,000 for all grand dukes), he began building a luxurious palace for a future wife, as he wanted to marry soon.[104]

At some point during her visit to Russia in early 1885, Marie met Michael, and soon after he wrote a letter (in French, with his seal) to Marie's mother (fig. 27):

> February 19 [1885]
>
> Madame!
>
> I am finally sending you the glass for tea that I promised you long ago. I earnestly hope you will use this glass for your tea, and that each time you will think of your Michel, who is so

Figure 26. Grand Duke Mikhail Mikhailovich (from Wikipedia).

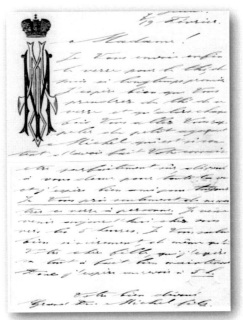

Figure 27. Letter from Grand Duke Michael to Jennie Van Zandt, February 19, 1885.

happy to have made your acquaintance and that of your charming daughter…This glass is only for you. I want to come to see you at 5 o'clock…

Michael must have considered Marie a very desirable candidate for his bride, and in fact a June 19, 1885, article in the *Paris Morning News* announced that

There is almost positive confirmation of the marriage engagements of two young American singers who have delighted Parisian audiences the past few seasons—Miss Emma Nevada and Miss Marie Van Zandt. Miss Nevada is going to marry her business agent, Dr. Palmer…

Miss Van Zandt appears to have conquered something more than the mere public during her visit to St. Petersburg, for she has won the heart of one of the Grand Dukes of the Russian Imperial House… The name of the royal suitor is not given, but he has followed her to London, where the engagement took place…[105]

This report was cited in *Le Figaro* the next day, but ended with the caveat "*Se non e vero, e ben trovato*"[106] ("If it is not true, it is well founded"). Miss Nevada did marry Palmer in October of that year, but Marie's letter to *Le Figaro* three days later made it clear that the rumor was not true of her!

London, 23 June 1885
Dear Sir,
I beg you to deny vigorously my alleged betrothal to a Russian Grand Duke. There is not a word of truth in that story.
Marie Van Zandt[107]

In spite of this, Michael's attention to Marie continued and seems to have become particularly ardent during her stay in Russia in early 1886.

Following this, he sent at least three telegrams to Marie while she was recuperating in Bavaria from the typhoid fever she had contracted in Russia. On March 31, 1886, right after she left Saint Petersburg, he wrote to her in Augsburg:

> I hope you arrived safely? How is your health, poor Mignon? Much regret not to have been at the station to say good-bye again. You must understand why I did not come…[108]

This last sentence suggests that his interest in Marie was not welcomed by the Russian court, perhaps because she was not of royal lineage.

On September 8, while Marie was at the Hotel Bellevue in Wildbad, Michael sent her mother a telegram, saying

> I am desolated not to have received any news of the health of your daughter. I am expecting a letter, that is why I have not written. I shall be here a week, then I hope to greet you, dear Mignon.[109]

This indicates that Marie had not been corresponding with Michael.

On October 23 he sent another telegram from Saint Petersburg:

> I would be happy to know how you are. How long will you remain? At least long enough to send me a letter? I kiss your dear hands tenderly. Remember me to your mother. Take care of yourself. May God guard you.[110]

A year later, a long letter from Grand Duke Michael reveals that he continued to be very attached to Marie. It also indicates that they had had "charming"—and perhaps intimate—times in Paris and Cannes in the spring of 1887 following her recovery from typhoid and leg paralysis. For unknown reasons, she had apparently allowed the relationship to cool after that, and they had not been in touch since then:

Borjom
October 18th, 1887
My Little Duchess Wissie,

I cannot tell you, my angel, *what a joy and how happy I was* to receive at last the wire of "poor Mignon" the day before yesterday. It was…the best gift for my birthday. If you would know how much I thanked the Good Lord to have at last news again from "poor Mignon"! Just think, there were *five months* that I had received neither letter, cablegram, or wire and I had lost you *completely out of sight* and you can well understand, my little angel…*how much I was upset and saddened and anxious.*

I had already told myself that "poor Mignon" *would not want to know me anymore.* On the other hand, I was afraid that you would believe the same thing; the more so after *our conversation in Paris* before my departure, when you had told me that *for sure I would forget poor Mignon*…and I had answered you that *that would never happen, even if one day I would get married…*

I am distressed not to have received…your *portrait promised so long ago* and above all *your little photograph painted in the rose "smoking dress," my favorite costume.* May I hope, however, to have them some day?

My Lord, My Lord, when I think of our charming stay in Cannes and the *last days of suffering* in Paris—I know, tears come into my eyes when I think of it; especially the last evening…

What concerns me, as you see, I am *still not promised* [engaged] and I believe I will have to wait still a long time. I am sure, dear Wissie, that if [you] would only follow all the articles in the English papers, because everything is arranged, and if not that I will soon be promised…If you would only know, poor Mignon, *how much and how much* I have thought of you during my stay in London…[B]ut when again will I have *the happiness of seeing you*? I will give you *my detailed report*, as I have the habit of being frank with you. I have spent nearly six weeks in London and I left [to return to Saint Petersburg for military service] just before the jubilee [celebrating Victoria's fiftieth year as queen]. To pay court neither to Lady Dalhousie, neither to anyone else, I have not done it.[111]

Although this long letter does not directly propose marriage, it addresses her as "My Little Duchess Wissie" and expresses ardent passion—but it also seems to suggest he will likely soon be betrothed to someone else. In fact, he was reported to have made several attempts at marrying outside of the ranks of royalty.

In any case, their relationship apparently went no further; however, Michael and Marie maintained correspondence by letter and telegram long after his marriage in 1891 to the daughter of the Duke of Nassau, who was the granddaughter of the Russian poet Pushkin. Because this marriage was morganatic, Michael was forced to sever connections with the Russian royal family; he spent the rest of his life in London and Cannes.[112] Michael and Marie's long period of correspondence ended with a brief telegram to her in Moscow in 1899, after her marriage to another prominent Russian (which will be discussed in chapter 14).

CHAPTER 10

Career and Acclaim Continue, 1887–91

MARIE, PRESUMABLY WITH HER MOTHER, left Paris for Cannes in December 1886 and remained there into the spring of 1887. It was reported that she was

> as lively and spruce as ever, living in a lovely villa near Esterel and making brilliant echoes with a voice that has never been better. By good fortune her neighbor is Jenny Lind, who has become great friends with her and who treats her as her protégée. And, as a seed sown upon fine soil, it is certain that the young diva's talent will double in a short period of time. It is indeed unfortunate for Paris that Mlle. Van Zandt has apparently decided not to reappear there.[113]

In spite of her resignation from the Opéra-Comique, Marie was still regarded as one of the leading young opera stars of the time. During this period, as she later said, "I sang all over Europe…in Italy, in Russia, in England, in Belgium, everywhere." An indication of her continued fame is the February 1887 acrostic poem and elaborate pencil drawing by Fernand Strauss, author of *The English Gentleman's Pocket Guide to Paris,* in tribute to her portrayal of Mignon, Dinorah, and Lakmé (fig. 28; note that the banner indicates that she had added *The Magic Flute* and *The Marriage of Figaro* to her repertoire). Translated, the poem reads:

> Mignon, you are that strange little girl,
> A look of an imp but the smile of an angel;

Brought to life by Thomas, the forgotten masterpiece,
Brought to fame by Galli-Marié.[114]
You have given her a second life;
Van Zandt, by your talent you scoff at envy
After having sung Mignon and Dinorah
We come to applaud Lakmé whom you have created.
They are envious, modern aristocrats
After the great success obtained by Van Zandt.
We must swear your critics are tarnished.
In that creation, Miss Fauvette[115] achieves
All that was promised by her renowned talent.

Figure 28. Poem and pencil drawing tribute to Marie by Fernand Strauss, dated New York, February 1887.

Also in Marie's collection of souvenirs is another, but unsigned and undated, acrostic poem in very fine English handwriting that reads (fig. 29):

Methinks thee a jewel in living form,
A goddess from a sea of talent born.
Radiant as the golden dazzle of the sunny skies
Is the glittering lustre of thy ever sparkling eyes,
Exciting admiration, heavenly, divine,
Vanishing earthly thought in feeling most sublime.
And to shape perfection in thy tiny feet
Nature did command all beauty there to meet.
Zealous gods did fashion them, inspired by art from high
And wafted their wing-like work to mortals with a sigh.
Nymph-like maiden—sweet being of gift and talent
Dare to accept these words in all their good intent,
Though they be sent thee without thy least assent.

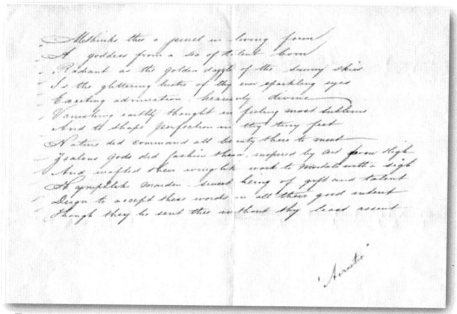

Figure 29. Undated and unsigned acrostic poem written in tribute to Marie.

While in Cannes on April 10, 1887, Marie was invited to lunch by Prince Henri d'Orléans, a young aristocrat who went on to become a well-known explorer in Siberia and Indo-China.

By early May she was completely healthy and could walk without a cane or brace, and on May 5 she returned to Paris on her way to London. While she was there, ten-year-old child-prodigy pianist Josiv (Josef) Hofmann (1876–1957) presented her with a photographic and musical carte de visite (fig. 30). Hofmann went on to pursue a very successful career, mostly in the United States, and eventually became head of the Curtis Institute in Philadelphia.

Figure 30. Carte de visite from ten-year-old piano prodigy Josiv Hofmann, May 17, 1887.

On May 25, 1887, the Opéra-Comique was destroyed by a fire that started with small flaming objects that fell on the stage just as a performance of *Mignon* was beginning. One hundred thirty-one people died, including many performers. Marie was not on the program and was not at the theater that night. There is no mention of her in the next day's newspaper accounts of the disaster; she is not mentioned until the end of a long article about the fire and its aftermath in *Le Figaro* on May 27:

> It is said that Marie Van Zandt has promised her help in organizing a benefit for the victims. The charming artist agrees to do it in the foyer of the Opéra. She has zealously seized the occasion that is offered to her to make a curtain call in remembrance of her old comrades at the Salle Favart [i. e., Opéra-Comique], and to reconquer at the same time the "bravos" of all Parisians.[116]

The reference to "old comrades" confirms that she was not part of the Opéra-Comique at this time. As described below, Marie did soon do a benefit concert for the victims, but not at the Opéra.

Interestingly, although Director Carvalho did all he could to help evacuate the theater and remained on the scene for days to assist in the aftermath, he was later convicted of negligence in the incident and imprisoned for three months. This may have been because an inspection just two weeks before had found that conditions in the building would make it difficult for actors and audience to escape a fire,[117] and he may have been held responsible for those conditions. He appealed, was ultimately acquitted, and was reinstated as director in 1891.[118]

On June 3, Marie gave a recital at the home of Baroness Adolphe de Rothschild. This was her first performance in Paris since March 1885. The account in *Le Gaulois* the next day read:

> Marie Van Zandt appeared yesterday at the home of Baroness Adolphe de Rothschild in this beautiful place on the Rue de Monceau, so often described as one of the most brilliant in existence.

Charming and a little nervous, the little American diva, wore a pale rose Empire gown with cascades of lace and a black hat covered with high black feathers. Welcomed by the bravos that hardly finished, she sang, with her bird-like voice, (which has become more robust), "Ecstasy" by Rubinstein; the mazurka in A-flat of Chopin, arranged for Jenny Lind, who alone had sung this previously...then came "The Butterflies" by Baroness Willy de Rothschild; and finally the bolero from *The Sicilian Vespers*, after which she was embraced by those present...The charming Van Zandt was radiant in her triumph.

While most of the guests were at the buffet, the artist had a heartfelt inspiration: "I cannot do for the victims of the Opéra-Comique what I would like to. I am not rich, but I have my songs, let us try to make some money from them."...She asked Mr. Campbell-Clarke, of the *Daily Telegraph*, "Would you let me use your home to do something for the victims of the horrible catastrophe?" Everything was arranged. There will be 200 seats at 5 louis each. "By this evening we will have the program and the names of the artists."

[There follows a partial list of the attendees, which included six princes, three princesses, two dukes, seven duchesses, six counts, twelve countesses, four marquis, two marquises, four barons, two baronesses, and one lord.][119]

The benefit concert was given just six days later, on June 9, at the palatial home of M. Campbell-Clarke, the Paris correspondent of the London *Daily Telegraph*, again attracting an audience of the highest ranks of Parisian society and raising 7,000 francs (fig. 31). Marie was highly complimented by the press for her generous gesture, her appearance, and her performance:

Delightful, Mlle. Van Zandt in her gown of pale blue satin and old rose. The cruel illness from which she suffered has left no traces other than a slight limp, which only adds to her charm. The diva did her utmost. In this exquisite voice which, in the low notes, has acquired a profound sonority, she sang with M. Bjorsten the duets from *Mireille* and from *La Traviata* and, solo, Chopin's "Mazurka" and the bolero from *The Sicilian Vespers*. Impossible to pay more amply her debt. And for that she was also acclaimed.[120]

Marie and M. Campbell-Clarke personally delivered the money to the committee overseeing the benefit fund.[121]

Figure 31. Announcement of Marie's concert to raise money for the victims of the Opéra-Comique fire, June 9, 1887.

Marie left Paris on June 18 for London, but we have no information about her activities there. In September she was back at the spa in Wildbad "in superb health"[122] and negotiating to give a series of performances of *Lakmé* in Nice. The king and queen of Brazil were in Paris in October and specifically requested that Marie sing pieces from three of her operas at a soirée given in their honor. Marie returned to Paris (from where is not clear) for this command performance.[123] She also gave a very successful series of concerts in Vienna in late December, and although she was hoping to play Lakmé there, she could not because another singer had been previously engaged for the part.[124]

By the end of December, Marie and her mother were back in Paris, but left for Nice on January 2, 1888, where Marie was to sing in *Lakmé* and possibly also in Ambroise Thomas's *Hamlet*. Delibes was present at the opening of *Lakmé* on January 21, which was Marie's first public performance in France since leaving the Opéra-Comique. It was attended by a "very aristocratic" audience, and Marie was very warmly applauded.[125]

Le Figaro announced on March 4 that Marie had signed with Maurice Grau, an impresario who brought many operatic stars to the United States, to appear in operas and concerts in America in the 1890–91 season.[126] For some reason, this did not happen, and her American debut did not occur until a year later.

Meanwhile, Marie's European career continued to flourish, and she departed Paris for Moscow on March 12, where she appeared in *Lakmé* and *Mignon*.[127] She remained a great favorite of the Russian court and society,[128] and it was at this time that she was presented with an exquisite coffee and tea service of intricately worked Russian silver and niello, inscribed to "Marie Van Zandt From your admirer N. E. Tarbeev Moscow 19 April 1888" (figs. 32 and 33).[129] From the quality of this gift, we can be sure that Tarbeev was indeed a great admirer and was wealthy, but he is not mentioned in any other of Marie's effects, and we know nothing about him. It was probably at this time that Anton Rubinstein, a very well-known pianist and composer and the teacher of Josiv Hofmann, sent Marie the musical note shown in figure 34 and that Marie was given the silver salt dish, silver plate, and gold pin shown in figure 35.

Figure 32. Silver coffee and tea service given to Marie during her season in Russia in the spring of 1888. Tray, courtesy of Susan L. [Van Zandt] Ferraro.

Figure 33. (a) Tray of the silver coffee and tea service; (b) detail: inscribed "Marie Van Zandt;" (c) detail: inscribed "From your admirer N. E. Tarbeev Moscow 12 April 1888." Translation, courtesy of Prof. Arna Bronstein, University of New Hampshire. Tray courtesy of Susan L. [Van Zandt] Ferraro.

Figure 34. Musical note from Anton Rubinstein (1829–94).

Figure 35. (a) Silver salt dish, (b) silver plate, and (c) gold pin with diamonds, rubies, and sapphire pendant given to Marie in Russia, probably in 1888.

Marie returned to Paris and appeared at a high-society costume ball on May 19, dressed as Mignon. The ball lasted until 6:00 a.m., and other guests included Guy de Maupassant, poet Georges Boyer, and former Prime Minister Jules Ferry.[130] In September, she passed through Paris from Hamburg and went on to spend fifteen days on the Isle of Jersey.[131]

Marie went to Devon, England, in October to give private performances of *Faust* at the home of Paris Singer, heir to the Singer sewing machine fortune:

> Accompanied by her mother, [Marie] is leaving for England, where she will sing...Marguerite in *Faust* at the chateau of Paris Singer... Forty invitees will be accommodated in the chateau, and many others in nearby inns. Paris Singer will sing Mephisto. Mlle. Van Zandt will sing Marguerite twice, and receive 10,000 francs for each performance. In addition, Mr. Singer will pay for all the costumes, which are being expressly made in Paris.

The article went on to say

> After singing *Faust* at M. Singer's, she will go to Lisbon, and after returning to Paris, depart for Russia and Constantinople.
>
> In several days, Léo Delibes will see Mlle. Van Zandt to ask that she create the title role of *Cassia* which he has nearly completed for the Opéra-Comique. Refusal is certain. She is determined not to sing any more in Paris...although she has received many tempting offers from French directors.[132]

Her refusal to sing in Paris in no way impaired her career. By December 11, 1888, Marie had returned to Saint Petersburg to play in *Lakmé* at the grand opening of the Panaiff Theater. She was a huge success:

> Lakmé herself, otherwise known as Van Zandt, has just appeared to sing her incomparable *piquée* notes. From the time she arrived at the station she has been feted, and the ovations she heard there are a continuation of those she heard in the city. The public finds her as pretty

and charming as she was in 1885. She was recalled 20 times. The price of tickets has tripled. It was a great success.[133]

Marie then gave ten performances of *Lakmé* in Lisbon in December and January, and *Le Figaro*'s Lisbon correspondent wrote:

One lives on the remembrance of the 10 performances of Van Zandt, which were the hit of the season. A sparkling hit, prestigious, and which deserves all the flamboyant adjectives…[134]

Success in 1889 continued: Marie went on to Madrid in February, where she received twenty recalls in a performance of *Lakmé* that was attended by the Queen of Spain and Infanta Isabella.[135] In March she was doing that opera in Berlin, apparently in Italian, and was "called back more than any other artist.[136]" Her success there caused *Le Figaro*'s Berlin correspondent to wonder, "Why are we so stupidly deprived of hearing this delicious Lakmé in Paris? Has not this unfortunate suffered for long enough?"[137]

Marie did return to Paris in April, but stayed only briefly en route to London, where she was engaged to sing at the Royal Italian Opera (Covent Garden). She debuted on June 2 as Amina in *La Sonnambula* and also sang Cherubino in *The Marriage of Figaro*. The London public welcomed her and was somewhat disdainful of the treatment she had received in Paris over *The Barber of Seville* incident and its aftermath:

That the Parisians lost more than they gained by their unhandsome treatment of Miss Marie Van Zandt we have always thought; and our ideas on the subject are not modified since we have had an opportunity of hearing "the spoilt child of the Opera Comique" on the London boards.[138]

And as in her London debut a decade ago, most of the critics had nothing but praise:

Her experience on the Opéra-Comique stage has given her confidence, while it has in no respect impaired the beauty or freshness of her voice, in which throughout its large compass no trace of unevenness is found, while her scale singing is simply perfect. The ease and spontaneity with which her brilliant passages are delivered give her rendering of [Amina]...unusual charm. Mlle. Van Zandt, as the mischievous page Cherubino, won all hearts by the charm of her acting... Her "Voi che sapete" was sung with delightful freshness and purity of voice, and she has the invaluable gift of being able to look extremely like a boy, and a very naughty boy.[139]

A more ideally perfect embodiment [of Amina] we have seldom met with...Her voice has gained in power without loss of sympathetic quality; while in its use the...effects of expression and of technical skill belong to a high order of art...Miss Van Zandt did all her work with high intelligence, excellence of method, and strength of charm. She was frequently applauded.[140]

La Sonnambula...served as a happy means for display of the well-trained vocal powers of the gifted artist. Her voice has improved in richness of quality, and has lost none of that sympathetic charm which always distinguished her singing. The purity of tone, the neatness of her *fioriture*, the resonant utterances, the perfect form with which she sang...the clearness of her cadenzas, and all that could distinguish her as an artist...added to the pleasure her vocal performance created.[141]

Monday's performance of...*La Sonnambula* for the debut at Covent Garden of Mlle. Marie Van Zandt as the simple village heroine brought together another notable audience that in its large dimensions included...the Princess of Wales and the young princesses, the Marquis of Salisbury, Lord Charles Beresford, and General Boulanger. Mlle. Van Zandt...was a charmingly natural figure amid the pastoral surroundings of the opera, [with] the freshness of her bright clear voice and her wonderfully delicate vocalization, with those marvelously sustained high notes so true even to their last vibration...[142]

> [I]t is certain that a better Cherubino—either for archness of acting, grace of movement, or well-ordered vocalization—than Miss Van Zandt, it would be difficult to find.[143]

> [As Amina], Miss Van Zandt fairly captivated her audience…It is always delightful to hear a voice so fresh and full of sympathetic charm, that never by any chance sounds a shade sharp or a shade flat, that can sing a scale or a shake without fault, and render the most difficult *fioritura* with unfailing neatness and grace.[144]

> Once more she is with us, singing with wonderful vigor, and acting with marvelous "go" her old part, Amina in *la Sonnambula*. She has grown into a most gifted and charming lady…Mlle. Marie was the most delightful Cherubino I have ever seen.…Her singing was faultless, and her acting was not only naughty, but more than nice.[145]

However, the praise this time was not totally unalloyed:

> Mlle. Van Zandt acted [Amina] with her customary *naiveté*, and sang florid passages with purity of intonation and considerable fluency of execution, frequently winning applause. She should guard against her tendency to employ anticipatory notes when attacking some of the exceptionally high notes in which she excels, and she may also be recommended to appear less conscious of the…audience. The beautiful "Ah! Non credea" in Act III was too evidently sung "at" the audience, and was devoid of passion…but her fluent execution and the crystalline quality of her upper notes justified the prominent position she holds among *soprani leggieri*.[146]

There is little information about Marie's activities for the rest of 1889 and most of 1890. She vacationed in Marienbad, Germany, with her mother in August 1889,[147] and in late October it was announced that she was in Paris and had been engaged for a winter tour (where was not stated) in which she would sing Ophelia in *Hamlet* and Catarina in *The Star of the North* for the first time.[148] One source says she sang in Budapest at this time.[149]

On April 21, 1890, the *New York Times* reported that Marie was planning a tour of the United States for the 1891–92 season.[150] In November, *Le Figaro*'s Russian correspondent noted that Marie would be coming to Saint Petersburg in December:

> She will debut in *Lakmé* and will sing the roles of Mignon, Lucie, Dinorah, Juliette, Rosina, etc.…Marie sang five years ago in St. Petersburg at the Imperial Theatre, where she was an immense success. She was also heard at Gatchina [one of the imperial palaces]; the Tsarina and the Tsar are very fond of her. The voice of the young diva has gained in power; people are impatiently waiting for her, because the public adore her.[151]

On December 22 the paper reported, "Yesterday, first presentation of *Lakmé*. House packed, very great success. Mlle. Van Zandt was recalled 20 times."[152] However, a report of another distressing onstage incident appeared in *Le Figaro* later that season:

> We would prefer not to speak of an unfortunate incident involving Van Zandt in St. Petersburg, hoping there was no truth to the report that while playing in *Mignon* she sang an air from *Lakmé*. We telegraphed Russia and the report we received unfortunately removed all doubt. It is in fact true.[153]

The report soon reached America, and Marie's brother Tony immediately hired an attorney to look into it. That attorney soon concluded that the story was false and "was of the opinion that Miss Van Zandt's approaching American tour might have had something to do with [it]."[154] On February 25, 1891, *Le Figaro* reported having a letter from Marie denying the rumor[155], and on April 10 it printed a translation of a Russian legal affidavit swearing that

> the news published in St. Petersburg and in Parisian newspapers concerning the following facts, which have been attributed to the artist

Marie Van Zandt on the stage of the Petit-Theatre during a performance of the opera *Mignon* are totally denied, and that 1) Mlle. Van Zandt did not sing an air from *Lakmé* while the orchestra played *Mignon*; 2) Mlle. Van Zandt did not fall and injure herself on the prompter's shelter; 3) the presentation was presented from beginning to end in the usual manner without the slightest disturbance of the public tranquility or scandal; 4) the public did not demand that the curtain be lowered but had, to the contrary, expressed its approval of the artist and applauded Mlle. Van Zandt during and after the performance.

Signed by the Commissioner of Police…Translated by the official translator of the St. Petersburg Police Precinct. Legalized and signed by French Ambassador Laboulaye.[156]

The matter was apparently closed months later, with a French court seemingly supporting Marie's claim, but declining to award her significant damages:

Yesterday [30 December 1891], Mlle. Van Zandt pursued before the 9th Chamber the newspaper *Le Petit Parisien*, which she claimed as having defamed her [by printing that] "she has committed a scandal in appearing on stage in an inebriated state in St. Petersburg." Mlle. Van Zandt asked the judges to award her damages of 1000 francs because the report was repeated in French, American, and Russian newspapers. But after pleading of [lawyers] the Tribunal awarded her 25 francs plus her costs in bringing the suit.[157]

Marie must have been represented by lawyers in that proceeding, as she had arrived in New York on November 5 to begin her American tour.

In spite of this new accusation of onstage mishaps, Marie's success in Russia continued to the close of the 1890–91 season, where she sang in *Hamlet*, *Romeo and Juliet*, and *Faust*:

Mlle. Van Zandt sang Ophelia at the Chalapoutine Theater. She was given an enthusiastic ovation and a deluge of flowers and wreaths.

This success will suffice to deny the offensive rumors which have persisted to follow this young and sympathetic artist.[158]

Léo Delibes died in January 1891. At some point prior to this, perhaps when she left the Opéra-Comique in March 1885, Marie received a brief undated farewell note from him, saying

> Farewell, or rather, au revoir! With the most affectionate memories of your household. P.P.C. [abbreviation for *Pour prendre congé*, "to say good-bye"]

(fig. 36). However, Marie and Delibes may not have met again, as she did not return to sing in Paris until long after he died. In 1898 it was announced that the sculptor Marqueste had created a memorial sculpture in Delibes's birthplace, La Flèche, in the Loire Valley. "At the base of the stele supporting the bust is an image of Lakmé, playing an Indian mandolin. That Lakmé, everyone will recognize, is the charming Van Zandt, creator of the role."[159]

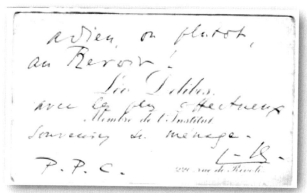

Figure 36. Undated (March 1885?) calling card to Marie from Delibes, who had been elected a member of the French Institute in 1884.

We do not have detailed information about Marie's activities for the summer and early fall of 1891. Presumably, she spent some of that time preparing for her oft-postponed and long-awaited American tour.

CHAPTER 11

American Tour, 1891–92

MARIE ARRIVED IN NEW YORK aboard the *City of Paris* on November 5, 1891, for an extensive tour of U.S. cities for the 1891–92 season. On arrival, the *New York Times* reported

> Sandy Hook [on the New Jersey shoreline], she declared, was to her like the beckoning finger of the Promised Land, and she should never, never want to leave these shores again. "And I feel such a stranger in my native land," she said pathetically. "To see all these houses, and think I am in New-York, and see the people moving about so briskly—that is such a change."…"And tomorrow morning we take a special train to Chicago, where I open in *Sonnambula*. I am frightened to think of singing before an American audience. Just think of it! Then, after five weeks there, back here to New-York—and possibly to Philadelphia. But that depends on the cash."…For a half hour Miss Van Zandt continued to absorb Americanisms, and pronounced herself delighted.[160]

The tour was under the auspices of the Abbey-Grau Opera Company and the New York Metropolitan Opera. Henry Abbey had been the manager of the New York Met in its inaugural season of 1883–84, and he and Maurice Grau were co-managers until 1897. During the tour Marie appeared in *Martha, Mignon, Don Giovanni, The Pardon of Ploermel* (*Dinorah*), *Lakmé*, and *Hamlet*; a complete listing of the performances is given in appendix B.

The tour began in Chicago on November 13, just eight days after her arrival, where she was "a great triumph" as Amina in *La Sonnambula*. The

Chicago Daily News review was as ecstatic, and as expert, as any she had received in Europe:

> What in the world can one say to exactly describe the lovely Van Zandt? She is like a stray melodious fairy. She is little, piquant, and altogether delicious. Her voice, sweet as lilac perfume, with every tone clear and steady…She is seductively tiny, with a naive, innocent roguery lighting up her pretty face and bubbling over in her acting. Brown babyish hair floats around her dimpled shoulders and waves over her low forehead and pink ears. Her nose is mischievous and her eyes blue as the Danube. I never saw so small a hand in grand opera nor so white and slim a throat. If she could not sing this fascinating little creature would own Chicago in a week. But she can sing most beautifully. Her voice is a light, high soprano of infinitesimal width but wonderful timbre and quality. It is splendidly trained in the Italian method. Stretched like fine silver wire to unattainable notes in alto, held in unerring abeyance through staccato cadenzas, chromatic octaves and intricate appogiaturas. Mlle. Van Zandt's voice is small but infinitely pure, sweet and flexible. The trill is not electric but correct and facile. In Amina she exhibits wonderful accuracy in attack and vocal contrapuntion [sic]. There are so many sudden leaps from chest to bell-like head tones that exquisite pose is absolutely imperative…Marie is her mamma's own girl about saving her dainty voice and the coquettish, ingenuous methods she assumes to hoodwink an enchanted audience is something rapturously artistic. She is a consummate natural actress with a bubbling of delicate comedy very rare and attractive. Poor, distorted Amina seldom finds so charming an interpreter…[161]

The *New York Times* review was equally positive:

> The first appearance of Mlle. Van Zandt in her native land was the significant feature of Friday night's performance, when "La Sonnambula" was given. She was accorded a very hearty welcome.

She made a delightful Amina, her acting being marked by naturalness and artlessness. Her entire freedom from mannerisms makes her impersonation doubly agreeable. She has a lyric soprano voice, not wide in compass, but round and delicately sympathetic, very flexible, and fine in its quality. Her method is perfect, and a voice better adapted to coloratura music could not be found. She has the true artistic instinct and her work throughout was characterized by the greatest delicacy and taste.[162]

Performances of *La Sonnambula* (three), *Dinorah* (one), *Martha* (two), *Mignon* (one), and *Don Giovanni* (one) were given in Chicago, with one side trip to give *La Sonnambula* in Louisville, Kentucky, on December 8. The next day she was back in Chicago as part of a "Gala Performance" to sing Rosina in Act II of *The Barber of Seville*—the very part in which she had faltered so disastrously in Paris in 1884!

The last Chicago performance was on December 11, following which the company returned to New York, where Marie made her New York Metropolitan Opera debut in *La Sonnambula* on December 21. After a break for the holidays, she sang *Martha* at the Met on January 2 and *Mignon* in Brooklyn on the fifth.

The first New York review we have is for her next performance of *Mignon* at the Met on January 8; it was less than ecstatic:

[N]o great amount of praise can be given to the performance. It had its happy moments, but they were fleeting. When they did come they were decidedly enjoyable…Mlle. Marie Van Zandt was a demure Mignon. Her voice is too small for the Metropolitan, and perhaps it may be as well to add, out of respect for the inviolability of truth, that her style is also too small. Her singing of the air generally known by its French title, "Connais tu le pays," was almost wholly devoid of expression. In the Styrian aria of the second act, when she had opportunities for ornamental work, she acquitted herself with greater credit and received a demand for an encore.[163]

Interestingly, a brief note in the *New York Times* of January 10 says, "At a Seidl Society [of Brooklyn] Concert the last act of Gotterdammerung was given with Marie Van Zandt singing Brunhilda."[164] This is the only time we know of that Marie sang Wagner—and it is amazing to realize that she either learned the part or was able to recall it while in the midst of a multi-city tour in which she sang seven other parts (see appendix B)!

Marie sang in *Don Giovanni*, *Mignon*, and *Dinorah* at the Met into mid-February. In spite of her American origins and European acclaim, subsequent reviews of the operas of Marie's American tour did not focus on her and, like the one just quoted, were generally lukewarm. For example, in the *Times*'s lengthy review of the January 18 performance of *Don Giovanni*, the only mention of Marie was "Mlle. Van Zandt was a diminutive and interesting Zerlina, but her voice was in company that was not to its advantage."[165] For her February 5 performance in *Mignon*—the role she most identified with and was so rapturously praised for in Europe—the *Times* merely said

> Only diplomacy and determination on the part of the management prevented a change of opera last evening, for both Mlle. Van Zandt, the Mignon, and M. Vinche, the Lothario, were suffering from some indisposition, and a printed apology for them was inserted in the programme. It may be said with justice to both singers that neither of them needed the protection of an apology, for they did their work with no less credit than at former performances of this opera.[166]

Marie again performed *Don Giovanni* at the Met on February 12 and *Mignon* in Philadelphia on the eighteenth.

The Met's first performance of *Lakmé* was on February 22. Again the *Times* review was somewhat restrained:

> The occasion was made especially interesting by the appearance of Mlle. Marie Van Zandt in the title role, which she was chosen to "create" by the composer. The young lady has not appeared here before in a part which was more advantageous to the display of her light and pretty voice

and facile execution. It is not exceeding the bounds of legitimate fancy to picture a more passionate and forceful Lakmé, but it would not be easy to find one more dainty. Mlle. Van Zandt displayed excellent command of staccato singing in "The Song of the Pariah," generally known as the "bell song," and was accorded a well-deserved demand for an encore. In her duets with Gerald she sang with smoothness and much taste. Altogether her performance was a pleasing one.[167]

Lakmé was given again on the twenty-sixth, followed by *Don Giovanni* in Brooklyn (March 1) and Philadelphia (March 3). The company then traveled to Boston to give *Lakmé* (March 15) and *Don Giovanni* (March 25) at the Mechanics Building Auditorium. We have no details about how these performances were received.

The penultimate performance of Marie's American tour was the March 29 presentation of *Lakmé* at the American Academy of Music in Philadelphia. Marie's reviews for this were similar to those she had typically gotten in Europe, but the overall production was faulted, and the audience was small:

There have been better performances of Delibes's opera at the Academy... than that of last night, but we have not had just such a Lakme as Marie Van Zandt's....[I]t has a peculiar personal quality, half wild, half fairylike, that is hard to define and impossible to imitate...And her manner of singing is correspondingly unique. It is the first time we have heard here the really marvelous upper register...Exquisitely sweet these long, limpid high notes are and wonderfully brilliant the clean-cut staccato...[H]er execution of the bell song was most surprising in its ease and fluency. The little introduction...fairly electrified the house. She takes the song with bewildering rapidity, but with a delicacy of enunciation that is consummate, and the...clear, bright notes that mingled with the tinkling of the bells derived a new sentiment from this eerie little figure...[168]

The production of *Lakme* by the Metropolitan Opera Company at the Academy last night was the least successful of the season from both artistic and financial standpoints. There was a disappointingly small audience and many of the singers were not up to their parts… [W]ith the exception of Miss Van Zandt, the cast was mediocre… [She] was the redeeming feature of the evening…She sang delightfully, and the "bell song" was a real treat…[169]

Marie's tour concluded shortly after at the Met in New York, where on April 5 she sang Ophelia in *Hamlet*, with an otherwise all-Italian cast. Interestingly, Adelina Patti gave her "last appearance in Grand Italian Opera[170]" in *The Barber of Seville* at the Met a few days later, on April 9.

We believe Marie's brother Tony was living near either Boston or New York at the time of Marie's American tour (his son Arthur was born in Dorchester, Massachusetts, in 1894), and although we have no record of it, she must have visited with the family when the tour was in Boston or New York.

CHAPTER 12

European Career Resumes, 1892–96

WE HAVE ONLY VERY SPORADIC information about Marie's activities in the four years following her American tour. She was back in Paris by May 1, 1892, and spent June and July in London. She was apparently still there in the fall of that year, when she received an intriguing letter from Count Albert Apponyi (1846–1933), a nobleman of an ancient Hungarian family, who served in the Austro-Hungarian parliament from 1872 to 1918 and who was called "the greatest living Hungarian" of his time.[171] The letter is in English, is dated October 27, 1892, and was sent from Pressburg, the capital of the Hungarian part of Austria-Hungary (now Bratislava, Slovakia). It reveals that this prominent European statesman was extremely fond of Marie, that they must have corresponded often, and that letters between them during her American tour had failed to reach the other party:

Dear Miss Van Zandt,

I am almost in despair about the contents of your last kind letter, which has reached me yesterday in the evening. How could you—but *how could you*—believe that I should leave a letter of yours unanswered? No pressure of business or of care can be powerful enough to make me deficient—I will not say in courtesy, but in friendship and devotion toward you.

Although Apponyi was not married at this time, there is no hint of anything other than a warm platonic friendship between them. But the letter does reveal that a recent letter from Marie had requested information about a Mr. Hempelmüller, who presumably was, or hoped to be, a suitor. Apponyi reported that

> I am but very superficially acquainted with [him], and I know nothing whatever of his pecuniary circumstances…All I know is that he is a very able and gentlemanly fellow, likely to make his way successfully through the world. His style of living is that of a well-to-do man, without any extravagance. But I think that [further] information can be had at the Austro-Hungarian embassy in London…He was a member of that embassy through many years when my late cousin was ambassador…and…he is still received…in my cousin's family.

We do not have any further information about Hempelmüller or his relationship with Marie.

As noted earlier, we have very little record of Marie's romantic life. But what we do have—the relationship with Grand Duke Michael documented in chapter 9, the elaborate gifts from Tarbeev (figs. 32 and 33), the above letter, and her ultimate marriage to Count de Tcherinoff (chapter 14)—suggests that her suitors came from the nobility and the upper levels of European society. The letter from Apponyi is one of several letters, notes, and signed photographs in Marie's effects from well-known people of the day, including Bismarck, President McKinley, the Prince of Wales, the King of Holland, and Henri d'Orleans (heir to the French throne) (appendix C). It would be intriguing to know more about this aspect of her life!

Marie was apparently busy singing in Europe, but not in Paris, for the rest of 1892. Her name does not appear again in *Le Figaro* until February 1893, when a brief note said, "Mlle. Van Zandt has just sung Lakmé in a city in the south of France [probably Nice] with great success."[172] Later that month that newspaper reported that she had suffered a double fracture of the leg when she slipped on the dock in Calais en route to London.[173] At this point Marie was once again singing for Carvalho, and the injury caused a six-month delay in her appearance in his production of Massé's opera *Paul et Virginie*.[174] In late March 1893, a newspaper reported that Marie, "whose health is as good as can be expected, although her leg is still in a brace,"[175] departed Calais for London. We have no information about her performances or other activities there, but in September it was reported that she would "probably" be playing in the new opera *Evangeline* at the Opéra-Comique.[176] This turned out not to be true, and she continued to avoid appearing in Paris; meanwhile, *Lakmé* was being performed at the Opéra-Comique, now starring Mlle. Petrini, a Swedish protégée of Christine Nilsson's.[177]

Presumably Marie continued performing in various European venues for the 1893–94 and 1894–95 seasons, but apparently not in France. However, France had not forgotten Marie and the incident that had caused her to avoid the Parisian public for ten years: In March 1895, *Le Figaro* briefly announced publication of a book of poems by Octave Houdaille, one of which was called "Miss Fauvette" and was "dedicated to Marie Van Zandt…and the cruel skirmish which her rivals organized against her and against her talent."[178] All we know of her until late in 1896 was that she was in Brussels playing Mignon in February 1896, where she attracted an "elite audience" at a memorial for Ambroise Thomas, who had recently died.[179]

CHAPTER 13

A Triumphant Return to Paris, 1896

DIRECTOR CARVALHO FINALLY CONVINCED MARIE to return to the Opéra-Comique. On September 7, 1896, *Le Figaro* reported that

> On Friday evening, Mlle. Van Zandt signed with Carvalho for an engagement from November 20th to January 20th for a series of performances of *Lakmé* and *Manon*, which she will sing for the first time.[180]

The city had missed her, and her return was much anticipated; that same day *Le Figaro*'s "Notes of a Parisian" column regretted that the public had greatly over-reacted to the *Barber of Seville* incident and subsequent turmoil and that during her absence

> she was applauded by the Belgians, the Germans, the Russians, the English, by Europe, and by America. We, meanwhile, had Mme. Jean Harding!
>
> Finally, all's well that ends well. We have sufficiently sulked… and we judge the moment has come to pardon Van Zandt for our own stupidity…[W]e have lost 10 to 12 years of her pretty voice…There is no reason for enduring this for 10 or 15 more years, to let her have time to go to India, China, and Australia…[181]

One week before her appearance, Jules Huret of *Le Figaro* interviewed both Carvalho and Marie. He questioned Carvalho about the 1884 *Barber of Seville* incident, and the director recalled that

> Mlle. Van Zandt was found *sick* one-quarter hour before the performance. She had spent the entire day with the administrative staff; at 4:00 the costumier came into her room; at 5:00 it was the turn of the cobbler; her dresser had not left a minute before her entrance on stage; she felt vaguely indisposed; she had not even eaten that evening. For strength, she had taken a kind of potion of phosphorus, and as she entered on stage she said to me "I am afraid. I am sick." She sang her first air with great emotion, then she found herself absolutely paralyzed…The poor girl has enemies inside the theatre and outside who terribly exploited that moment of embarrassment…Now she will return to us as pretty and as much in voice as ever. And for that I am happy![182]

When Huvet asked Marie if she was happy to be returning, she answered

> Yes, very happy. For a long time M. Carvalho has asked me to return to the Opéra-Comique. I answered "Yes", but my friends made me so fearful of Paris that I always put it off…In spite of everything, I love Paris and Parisians so much…I have had, it is true, much success, but Paris is Paris, you know, and I am very happy to return to it.[183]

Two weeks later, the following long article by "Santillane" appeared in *La Vie Parisienne*, titled "Resurrection of a Nightingale." We reproduce it virtually entirely, because it describes the significance of this reappearance to Marie and to the Parisian audience, which had so enthusiastically launched her into stardom and then seemingly turned against her, resulting in her absence from the Opéra-Comique for eleven years. The article also explains more fully how the disturbances surrounding her March 1885 return to the Opéra-Comique got confounded with the Lang Son Affair:

> In a few days an American singer whose name recalls many notable reminiscences to old Parisians like me is going to reappear on the stage of the Opéra-Comique.
>
> Mlle. Van Zandt, in 1884, although quite young, was at the height of a glory that Paris awards quite easily to pretty women. She was called…the Nightingale or the Warbler…and the most aristocratic drawing rooms vied with each other with bank notes for the pleasure of hearing her sing…Then, all of a sudden one of those strokes of bad luck happened to the poor little one…On November 9th, 1884, as Mlle. Van Zandt made her entrance on the stage before a full house in the first act of *The Barber of Seville*, they saw her swaying, mumbling, while smiling mechanically, and no sound came out of the Nightingale's throat.
>
> I remember the turmoil which this caused in [the Opéra-Comique], which two years later had to experience tragedies more terrible, tragedies of fire. At first everybody pitied her. "She is sick. What is the matter with her?" and many went to the doors of the wings to ask some news of how she was. Then, all of a sudden, without ever having known who was the first one pronouncing the words, a rumor was started, going from seat to seat and then from box to box—"Van Zandt is drunk!" Thus the crowd undergoes, at certain moments, a certain magnetic influence of which the reason is impossible to discover…A word of slander or calumny passes over the boulevard like a cloudburst and destroys the life of a writer or artist.
>
> [On that] night…I arrived at exactly two o'clock in the morning at no. 4 Rue Christoph Colombe where the poor Warbler lived. I found her sobbing in the arms of M. Carvalho, who was consoling her, and with her little American accent I hear her still repeating "Oh, Monsieur, it is an infamy—an infamy!"
>
> But the thing had been launched. How much more cruel are the rivalries among artists or writers, than those among grocers or

notaries! The notaries and the merchants…envy only the money of their competitors. Those who speculate on glory seek to kill the reputation and honor of their rivals…

Paris has committed many injustices, and those who have been dragged into the mud sleep today in the Pantheon. M. Carvalho, who is an old shrewd one, and who had a great affection for Mlle. Van Zandt, was certainly counting on this change of attitude. Five months after, on the 26th [actually the 18th] of March 1885, he made the poor woman reappear on the stage, whose heart beat very fast when she entered the first act of *Lakmé*. There were a few whistles throughout the house… Nevertheless the applause dominated and except for a little rioting going on outside, everything went fine. But the second [actually the fourth] evening, the 27th of March, when Paris heard of the defeat of Lang Son—suddenly one saw the Opéra-Comique surrounded by a shouting crowd. A mass of demonstrators who had left to go yelling under the windows of [Prime Minister] Ferry stopped when they saw people assembling; there seemed to be a need for protesting in the air. The Prime Minister was very far away, so they cried "Down with Van Zandt" with as much energy as they wanted to cry "Down with Ferry!"…

[The] prefect of police arrived with some mounted police. They charged; there were some crushed people and many poor devils had to sleep in the police station. A policeman [later said] "We had to prevent, before anything, the crowd going in to the Ministry, and the affair at the Opéra-Comique was an excellent distraction. Every quarter of an hour one of us came out of the theatre and…cried 'There is Van Zandt!'…The crowd dashed at them and the guardians of the peace charged. And the same thing started again. That was sufficient to hold, the whole evening, a few thousand loafers around the Opéra-Comique. Paris does not know how to demonstrate at two places at the same time. Mr. Ferry did not see anyone.

Let us hope this time that the coming back of Mlle. Van Zandt is not going to coincide with any historical date, and that Paris will remember that, in spite of the cosmopolitan fools that are everywhere, that it was originally the city of gallantry. When one remembers that serious journalists discussed in [lengthy articles] whether Mlle. Van Zandt had drunk a glass of champagne too many, one realizes to what point this revolutionary and terrible Paris is a big child whose hands can do everything but amuses himself with noise and big words.[184]

The reappearance took place on December 2, 1896. It is very clear that Paris regretted the distress that Marie had been subjected to in 1884 and 1885, and once again welcomed her as a star of the first magnitude, as shown in reviews in both London and Paris newspapers:

> The performance at the Opéra-Comique…was of remarkable interest. The audience was one of the most, if not the most, brilliant I have known at this theatre…It is easy to imagine the emotion experienced by the young singer on reappearing after so long a separation before a public which…awaited her with impatience. The role [of Lakmé] was admirably chosen for this occasion, for Lakmé, before appearing, sings inside the temple, whence she gradually advances to…center stage. In this first number she was admirable, and as soon as she ceased singing the plaudits were unanimous and prolonged…The rest of the evening was an uninterrupted triumph for her. Constant encores and recalls greeted her…[T]he performance was certainly one of the most notable ever seen at the Opéra-Comique.[185]

> Mlle. Marie Van Zandt's reappearance at the Opéra-Comique this evening was…a veritable triumph. The Parisian public had been longing to listen once again to the magnificent voice of the gifted singer, and the utmost interest had been manifested in the event for weeks before…A more brilliant and representative house…could not have been found anywhere, and scarcely had Lakmé appeared on the scene, and once more delighted the audience with her sweet notes, when she was treated to a regular ovation…[I]t was with perceptible and very natural emotion that Mlle. Van Zandt received this homage to her talents and this evidence of cordial sympathy…Songs and duets were rapturously encored,

and the enthusiasm increased with every act. Mlle. Van Zandt is in splendid voice, and her charm of manner also won her much praise. It was a magnificent reception...There can be no doubt as to the great popularity which Mlle. Van Zandt had retained in Paris.[186]

The Parisian public, very gallantly, has just repaired the wrongs against Mlle. Van Zandt. It has applauded, recalled, and feted with good grace the Lakmé of former times, frail little exotic idol who has overcome pain and a cruel and inexplicable anger...It is exactly in the role of Lakmé, written for her with so much attention and detail by Léo Delibes that Mlle. Van Zandt has reappeared yesterday at the Opéra-Comique, all agitated with emotion, very anguished and very brave also, evoking the memory of the distant years when she sang with such...charm, so penetrating and true, in pretty crystalline sonorities and bird-like vocal acrobatics, music so correctly light, delicate, and picturesque. And by the magic of memory, the evening will not have been simply an evening of simple reconciliation, but rather an evening of success for Mlle. Van Zandt...[187]

Yesterday evening saw the reappearance at the Opéra-Comique...of one of the most original artists of her time, Mlle. Marie Van Zandt, creator of Lakmé, the one who left in this role such unforgettable memories that one can say she was never replaced...Useless to recall here the painful evening following which Mlle. Van Zandt had to leave Paris...[I]t has been given to us to find again yesterday this admirable Lakmé with all the charm and grace in which Delibes wrapped her...[188]

Writing in *Le Figaro*, a "Gentleman of the Orchestra" gave a more intimate account that captures more of what Marie herself may have been feeling as she made this second reappearance before the Parisian audience:

When Lakmé, frail and graceful as a vine, descends from her dressing room covered in her mantle of gems, nearly trembling and with ice-cold hands, she remains silent and reflective, with grave mien. One reads in the eyes looking at her the most encouraging sympathy. But she looks at no one, and no one dares trouble her.

She enters on stage; she sings her first phrases, and immediately the entire audience applauds with enthusiasm. Behind the curtain people...ask themselves by what extraordinary faculty, by what phenomenon of will, the artist is able, with that abominable fear, to make such admirably pure sounds come out of her throat! But she continues and the curtain falls on a triple burst of applause.

M. Carvalho awaited in the wings; the first words from Mlle. Van Zandt: "Are you pleased?" Her director kissed her in her ochre make-up, and said to her "Quickly to your dressing room, cover yourself well, do not speak..." And he guided her gently by the shoulders...

After the second act, of which the success is even greater, her dressing room is invaded by a crowd of friends: American, English misses and ladies who come to her to speak their emotions and their joy. Her doctor is there, near her. He has given her permission to drink a bit of tepid black coffee. People bring flowers...She speaks a bit, very moved. "Oh, yes, I am pleased." She says, "But what horrible fears, when I went on the stage, when I saw again my Paris public, the public which had so pampered me 13 years ago! 13 years! But I was so young then. I have become less emotional, I feel it strongly, now that I have matured, that I have become more of a woman."

In the aisles there is unanimity...People are happy to recall their memories: "She is not changed"...The stage manager, the vocal director, the conductor, around M. Carvalho...agree that they find the voice of the "American Fauvette" now has a bit more substance... And when the final curtain fell, I heard said beside me, among the applause and the curtain calls, "Well, Paris is going to repair one more injustice."[189]

Marie was interviewed in her apartment the next day by Adolphe Possien of Paris's *La Nationale*. His report was titled "The Day after the Triumph:"

I wanted to know the impressions from Mlle. Van Zandt the next day after a comeback that the majority of the critics agreed to declare triumphant; but where can the charming artist be found? At the Opéra-Comique the janitress, stern and unfriendly, like any janitor who wants to keep her dignity, declared she did not know her address. "Write to her here if you wish to speak to her," this unfriendly watchdog tells me, "and mademoiselle will see whether she will receive you." "But that will delay me a great deal!" "Too bad. Do as you wish."

A request for an audience then? No! My impatience to get the confessions of the touching Mignon does not allow me to submit myself to this formality, and I hurry at once to the home of M. Henri Carvalho. "Oh," exclaimed the sympathetic secretary-general of the Opéra-Comique, "the address of Van Zandt? I don't mind giving it to you, but it is too early. She retired horribly fatigued from the emotions of yesterday evening. I doubt she will see you." "Give me a note; perhaps I will succeed by disregarding the orders." "Try. Only I warn you, you are going to have to face an English maid who, by not knowing a word of French, will be less tractable."…Now I am on the way to Rue Clement Morot.

Indeed, the lady's maid, who examined me with a suspicious eye, appeared scarcely willing to let me pass. I implored her with my glance and it was only after a few seconds of reflection that she decided to show me to the parlor.

Oh, how many flowers! How many flowers! Everywhere; on the furniture, on the piano, on the window sills, along the walls, baskets of orchids and chrysanthemums—the room is transformed into a veritable hot-house, and the strong perfume…goes to one's head. The doorbell rang. More flowers are still arriving and it has been that way since early morning…

Finally, here is the artist, pale and features somewhat tired. "You see me exhausted," she said; "Nevertheless, I did not want a member of the press, which was so generous to me, to have taken the trouble to come to see me uselessly. What can I do to be agreeable to you?"

"Tell me your impressions the day after your return that everybody recognizes to be a great success."

"Oh, Sir! If you could know how happy I am! Words fail me to describe my joy. Just look at these flowers! You can see that the people have been friendly. My dressing room was literally filled and I wished that they be brought immediately here to my house. Their sight recalls to me the most beautiful evening of my life. Everybody was so eager to be attentive and the sympathy of my fellow artists went to my heart. Can you imagine that even the stage-hands came to bring me flowers! It was so charming that I could not keep back my tears."

"How did I sing yesterday? I don't know. It was as though I were in a state of hypnosis and I had to hear the applause of the public and read the morning papers to convince me of the good impression that I made. I owe thanks to all; to the orchestra of M. Danbé which surpassed itself; to the gracious public; to my fellow artists; to my director; to all—all!"

"There is, however, a slight shadow in my happiness, for did I not read somewhere that yesterday's audience was almost entirely composed of Americans?" "Oh, do not be mistaken, Mademoiselle, the house contained the cream of all Paris." "I hope so. Besides, a date has been set for the second performance and they will see that I intend to give all my energies to justifying the applause with which they welcomed my return. So there it is. I shall stay in Paris until the end of December. I shall leave in January to play *Don Juan* and *Rigoletto*… at Monte Carlo. Then I shall come back here to create *Cinderella*."

I left Mlle. Van Zandt after these words, still congratulating her on her great success. "Good-bye, sir," she said, smiling. "If you write an article about this visit, emphasize strongly my gratitude toward the Parisian public and my profound joy."[190]

Marie's triumphal return to Paris and the Opéra-Comique at the end of 1896 marked the peak of her brilliant and turbulent career.

CHAPTER 14

Honors, Marriage, and Retirement, 1897–1919

ALTHOUGH MARIE HAD NOT PERFORMED in the United States since her tour of 1891–92, it seems Americans were still following her activities with interest. Her papers include an autographed photo of William McKinley dated October 2, 1896, about one month before he was elected president. And earlier in that year, the following article, with a photograph of her as Lakmé (see fig. 9C), appeared in the popular *Munsey's Magazine* under the heading "An American Prima Donna." The brief article correctly summarizes the arc of her career and reports a talent—perhaps spurious?—for playing the banjo, which no European commentator had previously noted:

> Marie Van Zandt has made her reputation almost entirely in Europe; but for all that, she has kept a unique place in the hearts of those who have faith in American music and who believe that our climate makes fine voices. She was born in New York, and her mother, who was a clever teacher, gave her her first instruction. Even as a child she had a pronounced musical temperament, and in her early years she picked up a knowledge of nearly every musical instrument that came her way. The noises of the street, the organ that played around the corner, fascinated her. Her brain wove every sound into music. With a banjo she learned the trick of making others hear what had struck her sensitive ears.
>
> Her mother took her to Europe while she was still a child, and put her under Lamperti, in Milan. In those days—the early

70s—everybody went to Lamperti, and it was the American girl's dream to make her debut on the stage of La Scala. The beautiful child captivated everyone. She was invited everywhere, and asked to bring her banjo with her. It was she who introduced to Paris and Italy the sad and merry songs of the Southern negroes, as written down by Stephen Foster. Her debut was made in Turin in 1879, when she sang Zerline in *Don Giovanni.* She was immediately engaged to sing at Covent Garden in London, where she made a decided hit in *La Sonnambula.* A year later she was singing "Mignon" in Paris. She has made her home in Paris ever since, although she leaves it for long tours. Her greatest success in the last few years has been as *Lakmé,* a part she created in 1885.

A little over thirty, Miss Van Zandt is still at the age at which Melba made her first success.[191]

On December 28, 1896, *Le Figaro* reported that Jules Massenet had wanted Marie to play the title role in his forthcoming opera *Cendrillon (Cinderella)*, which was to open the following March. However, this was immediately contradicted by the report that Massenet and Carvalho had scheduled *Cendrillon* as the first work to be performed in the rebuilt Opéra-Comique, which would not open until 1898.[192] Neither prediction turned out to be accurate: The premier performance of *Cendrillon* was not until May 24, 1899, after Marie had retired from the stage.[193]

But Marie's brilliant career was certainly not over. The last performance of *Lakmé* for the 1896–97 season was on January 31, 1897,[194] and shortly after that, she left for Monte Carlo to appear in *Don Giovanni* and, for the first time, as Gilda in *Rigoletto*. She clearly continued to be more than equal to the challenge of new roles, as a reviewer noted that

> the delicious purity of her voice and the profound charm of her acting made Mlle. Van Zandt a totally exquisite Gilda. She evoked enthusiasm by the remarkable virtuosity with which she sang the aria of the second act. She was recalled several times and covered with flowers.[195]

In March 1897 Marie was named an "Officer of the French Academy,"[196] showing that France had indeed erased the memories of her onstage difficulties and wished to honor her among the most prominent contributors to French art and culture of her time. This honor, and a summary of her life and career, were described in an extensive article in the *New York Herald* of March 12, 1897. The article included considerable detail about the November 1884 *Barber of Seville* incident and the hissing on her return to the Opéra-Comique stage the following spring.

Marie returned to the Opéra-Comique on March 30, 1897, and received excellent reviews playing Zerlina and Mignon for the rest of that season.[197] Interestingly, in April she chose to be formally photographed not as Lakmé, the role created specifically for her by Delibes, but as Thomas's Mignon, "the role which she considers her greatest triumph."[198]

We have little information about Marie's activities in the remainder of 1897. Léon Carvalho, Marie's devoted mentor and director for her entire career at the Opéra-Comique, died on December 29 of that year,[199] but we have no report of her reaction to what must have been a great loss.

Le Figaro reported that Marie had been playing in Moscow in January 1898,[200] but that was the last of her opera seasons. The reason was soon made clear in this newspaper report of May 8, 1898:

> The marriage of Mlle. Marie Van Zandt, the celebrated singer, with His Excellency M. de Tcherinoff, was consecrated on April 29th in the Russian Church in Cannes. The civil marriage was celebrated in Paris on April 27th at the Municipal Building of the 8th Arrondissement. M. and Mme. de Tcherinoff, after taking their honeymoon in Florence, will be living in Paris. Mlle. Van Zandt has given up the theatre, but Mme. de Tcherinoff, who continues to passionately cultivate her art, will be happy to sing within the circle of her friends.[201]

One newspaper report recalled the stardom she had known in Paris:

> We have learned that the marriage of Mlle. Van Zandt was performed in the strictest privacy. Assuredly…the delicious singer could have had

all Paris at her wedding. Paris never forgets its stars, above all those it has consecrated and holds sacred. Joy and happiness to our Mignon, to our Lakmé, to our "Miss Fauvette"![202]

In her files are congratulatory notes from Massenet and Philippe Gille, the librettist of *Lakmé*, as well as the Hungarian statesman Count Albert Apponyi (fig. 37).

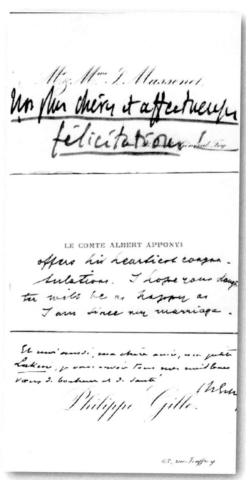

Figure 37. Notes of congratulation on Marie's marriage to Count de Tcherinoff from (a) Jules Massenet, (b) Count Albert Apponyi, and (c) Philippe Gille.

From this time on, Marie was known as "Her Excellency Marie de Tcherinoff." Her husband's full name was Mikhail Petrovich de Tcherinoff. In some reports he is referred to as "Count," consistent with the "de" in his name and the titles "His/Her Excellency"; one source says he was a Russian state councilor and friend of Tsar Nicholas II.[203] A brief obituary notice indicates that this was his second marriage; we have no information about when or how he and Marie met.

M. de Tcherinoff died on May 5, 1905; his passing was briefly reported in *Le Figaro* the next day:

> M. de Tcherinoff, the famous doctor and professor at the Imperial University of Moscow, died in that city. His second wife was Mlle. Marie Van Zandt, the famous singer.[204]

On the occasion of the 1906 revival of *Lakmé* at the New York Metropolitan Opera, Marie's father, James Rose Van Zandt, wrote a letter to the *New York Times*:

> On her retirement Miss Van Zandt married a wealthy Russian gentleman, M. Micha de Tcherinoff of Moscow, where she resided until his death some two years ago. She is now a wealthy widow in the prime of life and best of health, and divides her time between her villas in Paris and at Cannes."[205]

James Rose Van Zandt died in Connecticut in 1907. The following year Marie's brother Tony sailed with his children, Marion and Arthur, to visit their mother and Marie in France (fig. 38).

Marie Louise Van Zandt died at Cannes at the age of fifty-nine on December 31, 1919, following a "long and painful illness."[206] A lengthy obituary in the magazine *Sur la Riviera* recounts the beginning of her career in London; her great successes as Mignon and Lakmé at the Opéra-Comique; her acclaim throughout Europe (interestingly, Russia was not specifically mentioned); the *Barber of Seville* incident, which it called "an odious plot;" the subsequent Lang Son Affair; her triumphant return to the Opéra-Comique in 1896; and her marriage and retirement. It concluded with:

> [I]f something were needed to confirm the facts we have written here, it is the authentic excerpt from a letter to the famous singer from President Grévy, a letter which she kept up to her death which said "Poor Van Zandt! You are the last victim of the Lang Son affair." In respect to her memory and to fulfill her last desires, it is essential that this be made clear. It is done now. Rest in peace, charming Marie Van Zandt.[207]

Marie's brother Tony and his son, Arthur, sailed to France to attend to her remains and estate. When they arrived they found that her sister Amelia's son, Freddy Meyer, had had Wissie cremated and had placed the ashes in a wall crypt at Paris's famous Père Lachaise cemetery—apparently in accordance with Marie's wishes.[208] However, this was upsetting to Tony, who had wanted her body buried intact. Tony and Arthur brought many of Marie's effects back to America. Some of these have been shown in previous figures.

When the authors visited Père Lachaise in May 1983, they were disappointed to find that Marie's crypt was marked without her name, but only a number (urn 5890 in division 87). Recent Internet searches, however, show that an unknown person has had an elegant marble plaque with a vase placed on the crypt (fig. 39), a much more fitting tribute to a truly remarkable American musical talent who captivated London, Paris, Saint Petersburg, and indeed much of Europe for two decades!

Figure 38. At the beach in Trouville, summer 1908: (a) "Aunt Wissie" (age forty-six) with her dog; (b) "Aunt Wissie" with niece Marion Van Zandt and nephew Arthur Van Zandt; (c) Jennie Van Zandt.

Figure 39. Marie's crypt at Père Lachaise cemetery, Paris. Inscription translated reads "Singer, created Lakmé." (Birthdate should be 1861.)

APPENDIX A

Lakmé: Background, Synopsis, and Cast of the Premiere

BACKGROUND (MODIFIED FROM THE OPÉRA-COMIQUE website: http://www.opera-comique.com/en/seasons/saison-2013-2014/january/lakme, accessed on November 21, 2016.)

Lakmé, which is among the ten most frequently performed French titles, is also one of the most characteristic works of the Opéra-Comique. Its premiere was an instant success like *Mignon* and *Manon*—unlike *Carmen*, which the institution endeavored to revive the same year.

Lakmé was the fruit of negotiations between the director of the Opéra-Comique, Léon Carvalho, and the composer, Léo Delibes, then at the peak of his career. They were joined by three librettists, Delibes's faithful pair of journalists Edmond Gondinet and Philippe Gille (who signed himself "The Iron Mask" at *Le Figaro*), and the young Arnold Mortier ("A Gentleman in the Orchestra" at *Le Figaro*), who did not want his name to appear on the playbill.

Under the Third Republic, operatic subjects tended to be drawn from contemporary literature. Thereby, musical expression was enlivened, and audiences felt closer to the characters. *Lakmé* is a combination of two sources: *Le Mariage de Loti*, the second book by fashionable novelist Pierre Loti published in 1880 about the unfortunate passion of an officer and a Tahitian girl, and *Les Babouches du Brahmane* by Théodore Pavie, published in the *Revue des Deux Mondes* in 1849, about the revenge of a Brahmin priest humiliated by an Englishman.

In February 1881, Gille and Gondinet advised Delibes to read Loti: "The color, the idea of a wild passion battling with our European civilization are appealing to us," they wrote. Then Mortier found in Pavie's novel a way to divert the matter toward British colonialism under the reign of Victoria, the empress of India since 1876. An opéra- comique could not challenge the legitimacy of French colonization, resumed by the Republican government in Tonkin and Tunisia. Moreover, Anglophobia in France had never been so strong since Britain had reestablished a protectorate over Egypt. *Lakmé* followed a long series of works that caricatured the English, such as *Fra Diavolo* and *Carmen*, which display ridiculous examples of secondary characters. But *Lakmé* went beyond this, in that an Englishman was the male leading role in a boldly contemporary plot.

However, a prominent national stage such as the Opéra-Comique could not afford controversy. The imbalance of the colonial relationship, to which Loti was sensitive, was overshadowed by the romance of two familiar figures from the repertoire: the beautiful native girl and the foreign officer, both torn between loyalty and passion. As for the figure of the religious leader prone to fanaticism, a specialty of French bass-baritones, it is common to opera and opéra comique.

Synopsis

[From *Opera News* (published by the Metropolitan Opera Guild, Inc.), vol. 11, No. 5, November 18, 1946, p.18-19.]

Act i

The ancient Brahmin priest Nilakantha welcomes the faithful to his temple, hidden in the forest for protection from the soldiers of the British occupation of India. When his daughter Lakmé has finished her devotions, the old man dismisses his congregation and follows them to the city, entrusting the young girl to the slaves Hadji and Mallika. Lakmé and her maid Mallika, delighting in the freshness of the morning (the Flower Duet:

"Viens, Mallika, les lianes en fleurs…Sous le dôm épais le jasmin"), wander down the nearby stream.

The British Viceroy's daughters, Ellen and Rose, their chaperone Mrs. Benson, and two English officers, Gerald and Frederic, come upon the temple in their morning stroll. Finding Lakmé's jewels, they beg Gerald to remain and sketch them. Left alone, he hesitates ("Fille de ma caprice") and conceals himself when Lakmé returns, musing on a strange happiness that fills her heart ("Pourquoi dans le grand bois"). Seeing Gerald, she dismisses the slaves and joins him in a rapturous duet ("C'est le dieu de la jeunesse"). Nilakantha interrupts their idyll, crying vengeance on the fleeing intruder, who escapes into the forest.

Act 2

The public square of a Hindu city is thronged by merchants and tourists, among them the English party. Nilakantha, in beggar's guise, forces his daughter to sing a ballad (the famous Bell Song: "Par les dieux inspires…Ou va la jeune Hindoue") in order to attract the offending Englishman. As the fanatical priest plans to murder Gerald, the young girl tells her lover where he may withdraw safely to await her ("Dans la forêt près de nous"). A religious procession brings back the tourists, and Gerald admits his infatuation to his friend ("C'est un revue"). As night descends, Nilakantha lures Gerald away from his companions and stabs him, but Lakmé rushes to his side.

Act 3

Deep in the Indian forest, Lakmé guards her wounded lover ("Sous le ciel"). Blissfully they contemplate the happiness ahead, while distant voices echo from a sacred spring. As Lakmé departs in search of holy water, Frederic hurries to his friend, urging him to return to his regiment. The stricken officer is moved by the appeal, and when Lakmé returns, she realizes that she has lost him. Excited by the sound of martial music in the distance, he does not see her pluck a deadly blossom from the nearby datura tree and raise its petals to her lips. Together they consecrate their love ("Qu'autour de nous"). Nilakantha arrives as Lakmé falls dying, protesting that now she has expiated her lover's offense, while the ancient priest declares her immortal.

Premiere Cast (from Wikipedia: https://en.wikipedia.org/wiki/Lakmé, November 21, 2016.)

Conductor: Jules Danbé

Role	Voice Type	Premiere Cast
Lakmé, a priestess, daughter of Nilakantha	Coloratura soprano	Marie Van Zandt
Gérald, a British army officer	Tenor	Jean-Alexandre Talazac
Nilakantha, a Brahmin priest	Bass	Cobalet
Frédéric, officer friend of Gérald	Baritone	Barré
Mallika, slave of Lakmé	Mezzo-soprano	Elisa Frandin
Hadji, slave of Nilakantha	Tenor	Chennevière
Miss Ellen, fiancée of Gérald	Soprano	Rémy
Miss Rose, companion of Ellen	Soprano	Molé-Truffier
Mistress Benson, a governess	Mezzo-soprano	Pierron
Fortune teller (*Un Domben*)	Tenor	Teste
A Chinese merchant	Tenor	Davoust
Le Kouravar	Baritone	Bernard
Chorus: Officers, ladies, merchants, Brahmins, musicians		

APPENDIX B

List of Performances of American Tour

from New York Metropolitan Opera website:
http://archives.mdetoperafamily.org/archives/scripts/cgiip.exe/
Wservic…November 21, 2016.

Date	Venue	Opera (Part)
November 13, 1891	Chicago Auditorium	*La Sonnambula* (Amina)
November 18, 1891	Chicago Auditorium	*Dinorah* (Dinorah)
November 21, 1891	Chicago Auditorium	*La Sonnambula* (Amina)
November 28, 1891	Chicago Auditorium	*Martha* (Lady Harriet)
November 30, 1891	Chicago Auditorium	*Mignon* (Mignon)
December 5, 1891	Chicago Auditorium	*Don Giovanni* (Zerlina)
December 8, 1891	Louisville	*La Sonnambula* (Amina)
December 9, 1891	Chicago Auditorium	*Barber of Seville** (Rosina)
December 11, 1891	Chicago Auditorium	*Martha* (Lady Harriet)
December 21, 1891	New York Metropolitan Opera	*La Sonnambula* (Amina)
January 2, 1892	New York Metropolitan Opera	*Martha* (Lady Harriet)
January 5, 1892	Brooklyn	*Mignon* (Mignon)

* Act 2 only, as part of a "Gala Performance"

January 8, 1892	New York Metropolitan Opera	*Mignon* (Mignon)
January 18, 1892	New York Metropolitan Opera	*Don Giovanni* (Zerlina)
January 23, 1892	New York Metropolitan Opera	*Don Giovanni* (Zerlina)
January 29, 1892	New York Metropolitan Opera	*Dinorah* (Dinorah)
February 5, 1892	New York Metropolitan Opera	*Mignon* (Mignon)
February 12, 1892	New York Metropolitan Opera	*Don Giovanni* (Zerlina)
February 18, 1892	Philadelphia Academy of Music	*Mignon* (Mignon)
February 22, 1892	New York Metropolitan Opera	*Lakmé* (Lakmé)
February 26, 1892	New York Metropolitan Opera	*Lakmé* (Lakmé)
March 1, 1892	New York Metropolitan Opera	*Don Giovanni* (Zerlina)
March 3, 1892	Philadelphia Academy of Music	*Don Giovanni* (Zerlina)
March 9, 1892	New York Metropolitan Opera	*La Sonnambula* (Amina)
March 15, 1892	Boston Mechanics Building	*Lakmé* (Lakmé)
March 25, 1892	Boston Mechanics Building	*Don Giovanni* (Zerlina)
March 29, 1892	Philadelphia Academy of Music	*Lakmé* (Lakmé)
April 5, 1892	New York Metropolitan Opera	*Hamlet* (Ophelia)

APPENDIX C

Notes, Letters, and Signed Photographs to Marie from Famous People

From	Article
Jules Massenet (1842–1912), French composer	Letter; November 7, 1883 (fig. 12)
Léo Delibes (1836–91), French composer	Musical note; December 25, 1883 (fig. 13)
William III (1817–90), Dutch king	Certificate; March 17, 1884 (fig. 14)
Princess of Wales (1844–1925)	Letter via secretary; July 11, 1884 (fig. 15)
Prince (1841–1910) and Princess of Wales	Letter via Lady Emily Peel; August 4, 1884 (fig. 16)
Léo Delibes	Note on calling card; after 1884 (fig. 36)
Grand Duke Michael (1861–1929), Russian nobleman	Letter (to mother); February 19, 1885 (fig. 27)
Sir Arthur Sullivan (1842–1900), English composer	Letter; May 26, 1885 (fig. 20)
Sir Arthur Sullivan	Letter; June 2, 1885 (fig. 21)
Prince of Wales	Letter via secretary; June 9, 1885 (fig. 22)
Adelina Patti (1843–1919), Opera star	Letter (to mother); June 24, 1885 (fig. 23)

123

Otto von Bismarck (1815–98), German prime minister	Letter; Fall 1886? (fig.25)
Fernand Strauss (18??–????), English writer	Acrostic poem and pencil drawing; February 1887 (fig. 28)
Henri d'Orleans (1867–1901), French nobleman	Letter; April 10, 1887
Josiv Hofmann (1876–1957), Piano prodigy	Signed photo carte de visite; May 17, 1887 (fig. 30)
Anton Rubinstein (1829–94), Russian pianist and composer	Musical note; 1888? (fig. 34)
Count Albert Apponyi (1846–1933), Hungarian statesman	Letter; October 27, 1892
Axel d'Adelsward (1847–97?), French industrialist	Letter; November 18, 1896
William McKinley (1843–1901), American politician	Signed photo; October 2, 1896
Jules Massenet	Note on calling card; May 1898 (fig. 37a)
Count Albert Apponyi	Note; May 1898 (fig. 37b)
Philippe Gille (1831–1901), French librettist	Note on calling card; May 1898 (fig. 37c)
Lucien Fugère (1848–1935), French baritone	Letter; Christmas 1898
Jules Massenet	Note; May 24, 1899
Jules Massenet	Note; November 8, 1906
Jules Massenet	Signed photo; December 1909
Adelina Patti	Letter; November 3, 1913

NOTES

"CB" denotes Marie's book of 1879-80 newspaper clippings; "LC" denotes a loose clipping; "DC" denotes a clipping downloaded from an Internet source.

"MVZ papers" denotes the private papers of Marie Van Zandt.

1   Un Sapontin de l'Orchestre, "La Soirée Theâtrale," *Le Figaro*, April 15, 1883, 3.

2   Quoted by Jules Prevel, "Courrier des Theâtres," *Le Figaro*, September 24, 1883, 4.

3   "Van Zandt County, Texas," Wikipedia, November 3, 2016, https://en.wikipedia.org/wiki/Van Zandt County Texas.

4   Un Sapontin de l'Orchestre, "La Soirée Theâtrale," *Le Figaro*, April 3, 1883, 3.

5   "Derniers Hommages," *Sur la Riviera*, January 11, 1920, 1.

6   "Groton, Massachusetts," Wikipedia, November 4, 2016, https.en.wikipedia.org/wiki/Groton, Massachusetts.

7   Virginia A. May, *Groton Houses: Some Notes on the History of Old Homesteads in Groton, Massachusetts,* Groton Historical Society (1978), 117. The quotation is attributed to one Dr. Green. We thank Marlene Kenney of the Groton Town Clerk's office for discovering this connection.

8   Some sources give 1858 as her birth year and Texas as her birthplace, but Marion Van Zandt's notes state that Marie was born on Willoughby Street in Brooklyn on October 16, 1861.

9   *New York Times*, September 23, 1873, LC.

10   This date is four months before Jennie and Antonio were reported to have come back from Europe (see note 5). It is possible that Marie returned earlier with her father, or that the year reported here is incorrect, since this report was written twenty-three years later.

11   *New York Herald*, March 12, 1897, LC. Marion Van Zandt tried to confirm this report by querying local newspapers of the day, but was unsuccessful.

12   Unknown English newspaper, March 2, 1879, CB 34.

13   "Adelina Patti," Wikipedia, November 9, 2016, https://en.wikipedia.org/wiki/Adelina Patti.

14   *Gazetta Piemontes*, March 16, 1879, CB 3.

15   *Pall Mall Gazette,* undated, CB 3.

16   *London Observer*, May 4, 1879, CB 3.

17   *London Daily News*, May 7, 1879, CB 3.

18   *Manchester Guardian*, May 9, 1879, CB 7.

19   "The Theatres: Her Majesty's," *Bell's Weekly Messenger*, May 12, 1879, CB 11.

20   Charles-Simon Favart was a librettist in the early days of the Opéra-Comique, Wikipedia, November 9, 2016, https://en.wikipedia.org/wiki/Opera-Comique. One of the streets adjacent to the Opéra was rue Favart, and it was often referred to as "la salle Favart."

21 Lucy H. Hooper, "Ball at the Elysée Palace," *Philadelphia Evening Telegraph*, February 26, 1880, CB 35.

22 "Music and the Drama: Marie Van Zandt in 'Mignon,'" *Continental Gazette*, March 20, 1880, CB 30.

23 Etincelle, "Carnot d'un Mondaine," *Le Figaro*, April 18, 1881, 1.

24 E.N., "The Pardon of Ploermal," *Télégraphe* (Paris), May 28, 1881, LC.

25 Felix Jahyer, "Marie Van Zandt," *Camées Artistiques* No. 54, May 14, 1881, 1.

26 "Marie Van Zandt," *New York Herald*, February 27, 1881, LC.

27 "Opera-Comique," November 10, 2016, www.opera-comique.com/en/saison-2013-2014/january/lakme

28 Louis Besson, *Les Évents* (Paris), April 16, 1883, LC.

29 Victor Wilder, *Parliment* (Paris), April 17, 1883, LC.

30 Edmond Stoullig, *Le National*, Paris, April 16, 1883, LC.

31 Auguste Vitu, "Lakmé," *Le Figaro*, April 15, 1883, 2.

32 Louis Besson, *Les Évents* (Paris), April 16, 1883, LC.

33 "'Lakmé' at the Opera," *New York Times*, February 23, 1892, review accessed at archives.metoperafamily.org/archives/frame.htm.

34 Jules Prével, "Courrier des Théâtres," *Le Figaro*, January 29, 1883, 3.

35   Etincelle, "Carnot d'un Mondaine," *Le Figaro*, April 22, 1881, 1.

36   Robert Milton, "Sport," *Le Figaro*, August 18, 1883, 4.

37   Jules Prével, "Courrier des Théâtres," *Le Figaro*, September 15, 1883, 3; September 21, 1883, 4; September 23, 1883, 3; Albert Wolff, "Courrier de Paris," *Le Figaro*, September 22, 1883, 1.

38   Jules Prével, "Courrier des Théâtres," *Le Figaro*, September 24, 1883, 4.

39   Jules Prével, "Courrier des Théâtres," *Le Figaro*, September 25, 1883, 3.

40   Un Monsieur de l'Orchestre, "La Soirée Théâtrale: The Return of *Lakmé*," *Le Figaro*. September 27, 1883, 3.

41   Un Monsieur de l'Orchestre, "La Soirée Théâtrale: The Return of *Lakmé*," *Le Figaro*, September 27, 1883, 3.

42   Jules Prével, "Courrier des Théâtres," *Le Figaro*, September 25, 1883, 3.

43   Jules Prével, "Courrier des Théâtres," *Le Figaro*, October 13, 1883, 3.

44   August Vitu, "Représentation au Bénéfice de Mlle. Anaïs de Fargueil," *Le Figaro*, November 1883, 1.

45   Un Monsieur de l'Orchestre, "La Soirée Théâtrale: Van Zandt," *Le Figaro*, January 3, 1884, 3.

46   "Théâtres et Beaux-Arts," *Courrier de Lyon*, March 3, 1884, LC.

47   Jules Prével, "Courrier des Théâtres," *Le Figaro*, March 25, 1884, 3.

48   Jules Prével, "Courrier des Théâtres," *Le Figaro*, March 17, 1884, 3.

49 Jules Prével, "Courrier des Théâtres," *Le Figaro*, March 27, 1884, 3.

50 Frimousse, "La Soirée Parisienne, *Le Gauloise*, April 1, 1884, LC.

51 "Musique: Opéra-Comique—Rentrée de Mlle. Van Zandt dans Mignon," *Le Gaulois*, April 1, 1884, LC.

52 *Le Moniteur Universal*, April 7, 188, LC.

53 *La Liberté*, May 11, 1884, LC.

54 *La Gazette de France*, April 3, 1884, LC.

55 Un Monsieur de l'Orchestre, "La Soirée Théâtrale," *Le Figaro*, May 11, 1884, 3. The analyst, who was not told whose writing it was, was quoted as saying "I judge her to be elegant, trim, pretty, and out-going…She has obtained great success. Her voice must be very beautiful. One cannot doubt that she is an excellent musician…," etc.

56 Le Masque de Fer, "Echoes de Paris," *Le Figaro*, May 23, 1884, 1.

57 August Vitu, "Festival du Retraite de M. Pasdeloup," *Le Figaro*, May 24, 1884, 2.

58 *La Ville de Paris*, May 7, 1884, LC.

59 Letter from Charlotte Knollys, July 11, 1884, MVZ papers.

60 Letter from Lady Emily Peel, August 4, 1884, MVZ papers.

61 Un Fauteuil de Balcon, "La Soirée Théâtrale," *Le Figaro*, October 2, 1884, 3.

62 Peter G. Davis, *The American Opera Singer*, Doubleday, New York: 1997, 184.

63 *Le Gauloise*, November 11, 1884, LC.

64 *Le Soleil*, November 10, 1884, LC.

65 *Le Soleil*, November 12, 1884, LC.

66 *Le Soleil*, November 13, 1884, LC.

67 *New York Sun*, unknown date, 1907, LC.

68 Un Monsieur de l'Orchestre, "La Soirée Théâtrale," *Le Figaro*, March 19, 1885, 3.

69 Unknown English-language newspaper, probably from 1902 or 1903, LC.

70 Unknown English-language newspaper, datelined "Paris, Dec. 21" [1884], LC.

71 *New York Herald*, March 7, 1885, LC.

72 Un Monsieur de l'Orchestre, "La Soirée Théâtrale," *Le Figaro*, March 19, 1885, 3.

73 *Palignani's Messenger*, March 20, 1885, LC.

74 *Le Marechal*, March 19, 1885, LC.

75 This characterization proved questionable, as described below.

76 August Vitu, "Prèmieres Représentations," *Le Figaro*, March 19, 1885, 3.

77 *Times of London*, March 19, 1885, LC.

78 Jules Prével, "Courrier des Théâtres," *Le Figaro*, March 24, 1885, 3.

79 Charles, "La Guerre à l'Opéra-Comique," *Le Figaro*, March 27, 1885, 1–2.

80 Charles, "La Guerre à l'Opéra-Comique," *Le Figaro*, March 27, 1885, 1–2.

81 Charles, "La Guerre à l'Opéra-Comique," *Le Figaro*, March 27, 1885, 1–2.

82 Albert Wolff, "Courrier de Paris," *Le Figaro*, March 28, 1885, 1.

83 Un Membre de la Colonie Américaine, *Le Figaro*, March 28, 1885, 1.

84 Charles, "Chez Mlle. Van Zandt," *Le Figaro*, March 28, 1885, 1.

85 Peter G. Davis, *The American Opera Singer*, Doubleday, New York: 1997, 18

86 *New York Times*, March 28, 1885, LC.

87 "Mdlle. Marie Van Zandt," unknown London newspaper, March 20, 1885, LC.

88 Charles, "La Guerre à l'Opéra-Comique," *Le Figaro*, March 27, 1885, 1-2.

89 Philippe Gille, "Les Livres," *Le Figaro*, October 28, 1897, 4–5.

90 "Van Zandt a Scapegoat," *New York Times*, October 29, 1897, DC.

91 Charles, "Chez Mlle. Van Zandt," *Le Figaro*, March 28, 1885, 1.

92 Jules Huret, "Au Jour Le Jour: La Rentrée de Mlle. Van Zandt," *Le Figaro*, November 14, 1896, 1.

93 "Lakmé and Miss Van Zandt," *St. James's Gazette*, June 8, 1885, LC.

94 "Gaiety Theatre," *London Echo*, June 8, 1885, LC.

95 *Weekly Dispatch*, June 21, 1885, LC.

96 "Society in London: Notes from an American Lady in England," column in an unknown English-language newspaper published in Paris. Dated "1885" by Marion Van Zandt.

97 Jules Prével, "Courrier des Théâtres," *Le Figaro*, October 19, 1885, 4.

98 Jules Prével, "Courrier des Théâtres," *Le Figaro*, January 4, 1886, 4.

99 Jules Prével, "Courrier des Théâtres," *Le Figaro*, March 22, 1886, 3.

100 "Echoes from the People," *New York World*, August 2, 1886, LC.

101 According to *Wikipedia*, the Kaiserhof was Berlin's finest and most modern hotel.

102 C. Chincolle, "Chez Mllle. Van Zandt," *Le Figaro*, November 9, 1886, 1.

103 *Galignani's Messenger*, December 3, 1886, LC.

104 Alexander, Grand Duke of Russia, *Once a Grand Duke,* New York: Farrar and Rinehart, Inc., 1932, 149.

105 "Two Coming Weddings," *Paris Morning News,* an English-language newspaper, June 19, 1885, LC.

106 Jules Prével, "Courrier des Théâtres," *Le Figaro,* June 20, 1885, 4.

107 Jules Prével, "Courier des Théâtres," *Le Figaro,* June 24, 1885, 6.

108 Handwritten telegraph form dated March 31, 1886.

109 Handwritten telegraph form dated September 8, 1886.

110 Handwritten telegraph form dated October 23, 1886.

111 Handwritten letter dated "18/6 October 1887." Emphasis in the original. According to Wikipedia, Borjom (or Borjomi) is a resort in Georgia famous for its mineral waters and at this time was in the domain of Miche-Miche's father, Grand Duke Mikhail Nikolaevich.

112 Alexander, Grand Duke of Russia, *Once a Grand Duke,* New York: Farrar & Reinhart, 1932, 149.

113 Jules Prével, "Courrier des Théâtres," *Le Figaro,* March 7, 1887, 3.

114 Célestine Galli-Marié (1840–1905) was famous for playing Mignon at the Opéra-Comique in 1866.

115 "Miss Fauvette" was a nickname given to Marie by French newspapers.

116 "Incendie de l'Opéra-Comique," *Le Figaro,* May 27, 1887, 1.

117 "Incendie de l'Opéra-Comique," *Le Figaro*, May 26, 1887, 1.

118 "Léon Carvalho," Wikipedia, November 16, 2016, https://en.wikipedia.org/wiki/Wikipedia.Leon Carvalho.

119 "Mondanités," *Le Gaulois*, June 4, 1887, LC.

120 Parisis, "La Vie Parisienne: L'Obole de Van Zandt," *Le Figaro*, June 10, 1887, 1.

121 "A Travers Paris," *Le Figaro*, June 16, 1887, 1.

122 Jules Prével, "Courrier des Théâtres," *Le Figaro*, September 25, 1887, 3.

123 "A Travers Paris," *Le Figaro*, October 17, 1887, 1.

124 Walter Vogt, "Courrier de Vienne," *Le Figaro*, December 14, 1887, 4.

125 "Sport," *Le Figaro*, January 23, 1888, 3; Charles Darcours, "Courrier des Théâtres," *Le Figaro*, January 23, 1888, 4.

126 Jules Prével, "Courrier des Théâtres," *Le Figaro*, March 4, 1888, 3.

127 Jules Prével, "Courrier des Théâtres," *Le Figaro*, March 12, 1888, 3; May 14, 1888, 3.

128 The authors visited the Bakhrushin Theatrical Museum in Moscow in 1989 and were shown some thirty pictures of Marie taken in Saint Petersburg and Moscow, some in costume as Mignon and Lakmé.

129 Translation courtesy of Prof. Arna Bronstein, University of New Hampshire.

130 "A Travers Paris," *Le Figaro*, May 21, 1887, 1.

131 Jules Prével, "Courrier des Théâtres," *Le Figaro*, September 16, 1888, 3.

132 Jules Prével, "Courrier des Théâtres," *Le Figaro*, October 24, 1888, 6. Delibes never finished *Cassia*; it was later completed by Massenet.

133 Lydie Paschkoff, clipping from unknown newspaper, LC.

134 H. de Claverie, "Lettre de Lisbonne," *Le Figaro*, March 13, 1889, 4.

135 Jules Prével, "Courrier des Théâtres," *Le Figaro*, February 18, 1889, 4.

136 Charles Darcours, "Courrier des Théâtres," *Le Figaro*, March 25, 1889, 3.

137 J. de Saint-Mesmin, "Chronique Berlinois," *Le Figaro*, March 27, 1889, 4.

138 "Music and Musicians," *London Sunday Times*, June 9, 1889, LC.

139 "Royal Italian Opera," *London Times*, June 3, 1889, LC.

140 "Royal Italian Opera," *Daily Telegraph*, June 4, 1889, LC.

141 "Royal Italian Opera," *The Morning Post*, June 5, 1889, LC.

142 *London Stage*, June 6, 1889, LC.

143 "Royal Italian Opera," *Morning Post*, June 6, 1889, LC.

144 "Music and Musicians," *Sunday Times*, June 9, 1889, LC.

145 "Modus Operandi," *Punch*, June 15, 1889, LC.

146 "Royal Italian Opera," *The Globe*, June 14, 1889, LC.

147 Charles Darcours, "Courrier des Théâtres," *Le Figaro*, August 18, 1889, 3.

148 Georges Boyer, "Courrier des Théâtres," *Le Figaro*, October 26, 4; November 15, 1889, 4.

149 "Marie Van Zandt," www.Iipernity.com/doc/289582/41162638, November 17, 2016.

150 "Marie Van Zandt Coming," *New York Times*, April 21, 1890, 1.

151 Adrian Marx, "Lettre de Russie," *Le Figaro*, November 22, 1890, 4.

152 Georges Boyer, "Courrier des Théâtres," *Le Figaro*, December 26, 1890, 3.

153 Georges Boyer, "Courrier des Théâtres," *Le Figaro*, February 13, 1891, 3.

154 Unknown English-language newspaper clipping, hand-dated February 1891, LC.

155 Georges Boyer, "Courrier des Théâtres," *Le Figaro*, February 25, 1891, 6.

156 Georges Boyer, "Courrier des Théâtres," *Le Figaro*, April 10, 1891, 3.

157 Albert Bataille, "Gazette des Tribuneaux," *Le Figaro*, December 31, 1891, 3.

158 Lydie Paschkoff, "Lettre de Russie," *Le Figaro*, April 1, 1891, 4.

159 "Hors Paris," *Le Figaro*, December 17, 1898, 1.

160 "Miss Van Zandt Is Charmed," *New York Times*, November 5, 1891, DC.

161 Amy Leslie, "She Is an Ideal Amina," *Chicago Daily News*, November 14, 1891, LC.

162 *New York Times*, November 14, 1891, accessed June 3, 2016, via the Metropolitan Opera website: http:archives.metoperafamily.org/archives.

163 *New York Times*, January 9, 1892, accessed via the Metropolitan Opera website (note 162).

164 "Live Musical Topics," *New York* Times, January 10, 1892), 12, DC. The Seidl Society (later called the Symphony Society) was founded in Brooklyn ca. 1890 by Laura Langford, associate editor of the *Brooklyn Daily Eagle*, to promote musical interest among women. Joseph Horowitz, *Classical Music in America: A History of Its Rise and Fall*, New York: W. W. Norton Co., 2005, 158. It was named for Anton Seidl, a conductor of some renown, who was associated with the Metropolitan Opera and promoted the works of Richard Wagner, *Munsey's Magazine*, October 1895–March 1896, 730.

165 *New York Times*, January 19, 1892, accessed via the Metropolitan Opera website (note 162).

166 *New York Times*, February 6, 1892, accessed via the Metropolitan Opera website (note 162).

167 *New York Times*, February 23, 1892, accessed via the Metropolitan Opera website (note 162).

168 "Van Zandt's 'Lakme,'" unknown Philadelphia newspaper, March 30, 1892, LC.

169 "'Lakme' at the Academy," Philadelphia *Daily Evening Telegraph*, March 30, 1892, LC.

170 "Supplementary Season of Grand Opera," Metropolitan Opera House Program, April 5, 1892, 3.

171 "Albert Apponyi," https://en.wikipedia.org/wiki/Albert_Apponyi, November 19, 2016.

172 Georges Boyer, "Courrier des Théâtres," *Le Figaro*, February 4, 1893, 4.

173 Georges Boyer, "Courrier des Théâtres," *Le Figaro*, February 26, 1893, 3.

174 Georges Boyer, "Courrier des Théâtres," *Le Figaro*, February 27, 1893, 4.

175 Georges Boyer, "Courrier des Théâtres," *Le Figaro*, March 24, 1893, 3.

176 Georges Boyer, "Courrier des Théâtres," *Le Figaro*, September 30, 1893, 4.

177 Georges Boyer, "Courrier des Théâtres," *Le Figaro*, September 30, 1893, 4.

178 Phillippe Gille, "Memento," *Le Figaro*, March 13, 1895, 5.

179 Jules Huret, "Courrier des Théâtres," *Le Figaro*, February 17, 1896, 4.

180 Jules Huret, "Courrier des Théâtres," *Le Figaro*, September 7, 1896, 4.

181 "Notes d'Un Parisien," *Le Figaro*, September 7, 1896, 2.

182 Jules Huret, "Au Jour Le Jour: Rentrée de Mlle. Van Zandt," *Le Figaro*, November 14, 1896, 1.

183 Jules Huret, "Au Jour Le Jour: Rentrée de Mlle. Van Zandt," *Le Figaro*, November 14, 1896, 1.

184 Santillane, "Résurrection d'Un Rossignol," *La Vie Parisienne*, December 1, 1896, LC.

185 "The Paris Opera Comique," *London Times*, December 3, 1896, LC.

186 Unknown English newspaper, December 3, 1886, LC.

187 Jules Huret, "Courrier des Théâtres," *Le Figaro*, December 3, 1896, 4.

188 Dom Blasius, *First Performances*, unknown source, December 3, 1896, translated LC.

189 Un Monsieur de l'Orchestre, "La Soirée," *Le Figaro*, December 3, 1896, 4.

190 Adolphe Possien, "Au Jour le Jour," *Le National*, December 4, 1896, 1.

191 *Munsey's Magazine,* vol. 14, October 1895–March 1896, 480–81.

192 Jules Huret, "Courrier des Théâtres," *Le Figaro*, December 28, 1896, 5.

193 "Cendrillon," https//:enwikipedia.org/wiki/Cendrillon, November 20, 2016.

194 Jules Huret, "Courrier des Théâtres," *Le Figaro*, January 27, 1897, 4.

195 Jules Huret, "Courrier des Théâtres," *Le Figaro*, February 20, 1897, 4.

196 Jules Huret, "Courrier des Théâtres," *Le Figaro*, March 6, 1897, 4, said she was named an "officer of the academy;" "Van Zandt Honored," *New York Herald,* March 12, 1897, LC; said she was nominated an "officer of the French Academy."

197 Jules Huret, "Courrier des Théâtres," *Le Figaro*, March 15, 1897, 4; March 19, 1897, 4; March 27, 1897, 4; March 30, 1897, 4; March 31, 1897, 3.

198 Jules Huret, "Courrier des Théâtres," *Le Figaro*, April 20, 1897, 4.

199 Phillipe Gille, "Léon Carvalho," *Le Figaro*, December 30, 1897, 1.

200 Jules Huret, "Courrier des Théâtres," *Le Figaro*, February 3, 1898, 4.

201 Ferrari, "Le Monde et la Ville," *Le Figaro*, May 8, 1898, 2.

202 Unsourced and undated LC.

203 H. C. Lahee, *Famous Singers of To-Day and Yesterday*, Boston: L.C. Page and Co., 1898, 41–42.

204 Ferrari, "Le Monde et la Ville," *Le Figaro*, May 6, 1905, 2.

205 *New York Times,* December 30, 1906, 31, DC.

206 "Derniers Hommages," *Sur la Riviera*, January 11, 1920, 1.

207 "Derniers Hommages," *Sur la Riviera*, January 11, 1920, 1; Jules Grévy was president of France during 1879–87.

208 *Comoedia,* January 14, 1920, 3.

Made in the USA
Middletown, DE
10 October 2020